20

Merry Christmas

Brian + Brandy

+

Happy New Year

Love
Houston, Bonnie,
+
Lindsey

Home Again, Home Again

*O*PEN THE DOOR TO OUR COLLECTION OF SOUTHERN FAVORITES

THE JUNIOR LEAGUE OF OWENSBORO

Home Again, Home Again

OPEN THE DOOR TO OUR COLLECTION OF SOUTHERN FAVORITES

All proceeds from *Home Again, Home Again* will be returned to our community to further our mission of improving the lives of children and families.

Copyright © 2004
The Junior League of Owensboro, Kentucky
P.O. Box 723
Owensboro, Kentucky 42302-0723
270-683-1430
www.juniorleagueofowensboro.com

This cookbook is a collection of favorite recipes, which are not necessarily original recipes.

Library of Congress Control Number: 2003113744

ISBN: 0-9726424-0-4

Edited, Designed, and Manufactured by
Favorite Recipes® Press
An imprint of

FRP

P.O. Box 305142
Nashville, Tennessee
800-358-0560

Art Director: Steve Newman
Book Design: Jim Scott
Project Editor: Linda Jones

Manufactured in the United States of America

First Printing: 2004   10,000 copies

Dedication

The Junior League of Owensboro, Kentucky, would like to thank the people and businesses of Owensboro who generously support our fund-raising efforts and allow us to continue in our volunteer endeavors. Because of this support, the League programs have reflected nearly every area of community concern: child welfare, education, cultural enrichment, health, family services, the arts, and recreation.

Recipe For A Happy Home

4 cups love

2 cups loyalty

4 quarts faith

2 spoons tenderness

3 cups forgiveness

1 cup friendship

5 spoons hope

1 barrel laughter

Take love and loyalty and mix it thoroughly with faith. Blend it with tenderness and forgiveness. Add friendship and hope. Sprinkle abundantly with laughter. Bake it with sunshine. Serve daily with generous helpings!

Acknowledgments

Presidents

(during the production of *Home Again, Home Again*)

2001-2002
Joy Allen

2002-2003
Mary Dean Miller

2003-2004
Sara Hemingway

Cookbook Committee Chairs

Michelle Love, Chair   Jennifer Lyons, Co-Chair

Char Rhoads, Ann Watson
and Monica Zengel,
Recipe Co-Chairs

Christy Chaney and
Heather Clemens,
Art & Design Co-Chairs

Michelle Goetz,
Guest Chefs Chair

Laurie Campbell,
Sustaining Advisor

Christy Ellis,
Non-Recipe Text Chair

Stephanie Miller and
Jennifer Eubanks Wilson,
Marketing Co-Chairs

Joy Allen and
Kim Lashbrook,
Special Events Co-Chairs

Chapter Captains

Janet Rumohr,
Appetizers and Beverages

Karen Andersen,
Breads and Breakfast

Angela Woosley,
*Soups, Salads and
Sandwiches*

Tracey Danzer,
Side Dishes

Laurie Campbell,
Entrées

Shannon Hulse,
Desserts

Monica Zengel,
Just for Kids

Cookbook Committee

Sara Hemingway
Ashlie Iracane
Heather Lane
Kim Lewis

Michelle Mayfield
Michelle Parker
Emily Reynolds
Kristi Sigers

Jamie Szetela
Allison Truett
Kim Williams
Lynn Wiman

Special Thanks

UniFirst Corporation

Kelly and Lynn Wiman

Messenger-Inquirer

Trison's Gifts

E.M. Ford & Company

Chris Love

Smith & Butterfield Co.

Rhoads & Rhoads, PSC

Watson, Chaney & Associates

Sylvia Jones and Hadley Harrington
from *To Market, To Market*

Guest Chefs

Brian Jones, Head Chef
The Campbell Club

Reid's Orchard

Senator Wendell
and Jean Ford

David and Jenny Munster,
American Bounty Restaurant

Aimee Sanders-Garrard,
Great Harvest Bread Co.®, Owensboro

Chef Tony Rahill

Colby's Fine Food & Spirits

Moonlite Bar-B-Q Inn

Katie and Jon Brennan

To all active, sustaining, and provisional members of the Junior League of Owensboro, we would like to thank you for your constant support of this special project. You each took this wonderful cookbook and made it part of your home, and we greatly appreciate your continuous service in bringing it to fruition.

We especially want to thank all of our husbands and families who have supported us throughout this huge project. Without your never-ending support and assistance, we would not have been able to devote the time needed to make *Home Again, Home Again* the wonderful book it has become.

Financial Sponsors

Palace

Unilever Bestfoods North America

 Unilever
Bestfoods
North America

Estate

Old National Bank

Manor

The Past Presidents Club Members:

Joy Carpenter Allen	Marilyn Mills
Mignon Backstrom	Suzette Green Nunley
Biji Baker	Ruth Steele Reed
Beth Hoffman Best	Nettie Sweeney Rhodes
Jeanne M. Clark	Judy Moore Romans
Martha Fitts Clark	Eudora Vance Scott
Jane Martin Delker	Jane Stevenson
Becky Cruce Gordon	Eleanor Sutton
Suzanne Hays	Ann Lauzon Swinford
Sara Cecil Hemingway	Susie Walton Tyler
Mary Anne Howard	Linda Berst Wahl
Mary Ann Fitts Medley	Sharon Blakeman Wilson
Mary Dean Miller	Marilyn Field Young

Financial Sponsors

Mansion

Beth and Bob Best

Miles Farm Supply

Texas Gas

Winding River Health Care

Penthouse

Robert and Theresa Bahnick

Great Harvest Bread Co.®, Owensboro

Villa

Kerri Bradley

E. M. Ford & Company

Executive Inn Rivermont

Glenn Funeral Home

Kroger

Chris and Michelle Love

Owensboro Medical Health System

Roberts Motor Sales, Inc.

Sandra Watts

Wyndall's Enterprises

Condo

Dan and Karen Andersen

BKD, LLP

Canteen Service Co. of Owensboro

Daramic, Inc.

Independence Bank

Barbara Jarvis

Kimberly-Clark Corporation

Mr. and Mrs. David Lyons

Martin Custom Building, Inc.

Olivia Christine Miller

Stephanie and Fred Miller

Owensboro Community and
    Technical College

Owensboro Municipal Utilities

Radiology, PSC

Neil and Janet Rumohr

Dr. Robert and Janice Schell

David C. Scott Charitable Trust

Smith & Butterfield Co.

Trison's Gifts

Financial Sponsors

Playhouse

Jenny and Brad Anderson

Michael Austin, DMD

Dr. Mark and Carol Bothwell

Duncan and Laurie Campbell

Peggy and Voyd Clifton

Mimi Davis

Heather and Jason Estes

Cindy Hudson

In honor of Joyce Lyles by
Mr. and Mrs. J. Todd Inman

Christopher McCoy, MD

Moonlite Bar-B-Q Inn

National City Bank

Nation's Medicines, Villa Point

Reid's Orchard

Republic Bank & Trust

In honor of Sarah, Hayden, and
Andrew Riney

JoAnn Risner & Associates Realty

Liz Seibert

Karissa Shelton

Mr. and Mrs. Kirk Shelton

Anne Sheriff

Traditions, Inc.

Jennifer and Adam Wilson

Kelly and Lynn Wiman

Yager Materials

Financial Sponsors

Home Furnishings

Vicky Buchanan

Stacey and Garrett Carter

J. Edward and Gloria Cecil

Peggi Clark

Chad and Stacey Cowan

Joe Danzer, DMD

Rodney and Christy Ellis

For Chandler, Carleigh, and
Cailyn Fleischmann

Jana Beth and Matt Francis

Stephanie and Barry Frey

Steve and Tricia Frey

Mr. and Mrs. Vince Frey

Kristina Ghosal

Matthew and Christina Hayden

Susan Kay Heck

Kimberly Johnson and Randy Spaw

Heather and Sean Lane

In honor of our parents by
Chris and Michelle Love

Daniel Harrison Love

Jessica Nicole Love

Katherine Elizabeth Mellon

Alma Mullican

Shelly Murphy

Abby Lou Newman

Angela and Brandon Peters

Tammy Rice

Cathy and Tony Ringham

Mike and Lisa Sullivan

Amy Waggener, epwbooks.com

Jeffrey and Kimberly Williams

Martie Williams

Angela Woosley

Dan and Monica Zengel

Meredith Stone Zengel

Wade Stone Zengel

About Our Artists

Christy Chaney

Christy Chaney joined the Junior League of Owensboro in 2002 and immediately volunteered her services as an artist for *Home Again, Home Again*. Born and raised in Owensboro, Christy attended Kentucky Wesleyan College, earning a degree in studio arts. When not working as a fifth-generation funeral director at Glenn Funeral Home in Owensboro, Christy enjoys scrap booking, oil painting, and decorative arts such as furniture, murals, and faux finishes.

Heather Clemens

Heather Clemens, one of the artists for *Home Again, Home Again*, has always enjoyed drawing and art and is basically self-taught. As a child, she loved to draw and doodle on any blank surface. It all began when she was two years old with a bright purple crayon and the wall of her bathroom. Needless to say, her parents were not impressed with her artistic abilities at the time. She then moved on to closet walls, garage walls, or anything that was blank and begging for color. She still loves to paint murals on walls and has recently found that she enjoys painting furniture as well.

About Our Icons

To celebrate the twentieth anniversary of our first cookbook, *To Market, To Market*, we are including some favorite recipes as voted on by our sustaining members. These recipes are staples within many homes in our community, and we are pleased to honor *To Market, To Market* with their inclusion within *Home Again, Home Again*.

Throughout this cookbook, you will find a chef's hat beside certain recipes. These indicate our "Guest Chef" recipes that we are very proud to share with you. Many of these individuals or restaurants have a long-standing tradition within Owensboro, and we know that you will enjoy their recipes and their history included on the same page.

Brand Name Recommendations

The Junior League of Owensboro recommends using the following brands when preparing the recipes in *Home Again, Home Again*: Bertolli olive oil, Breyers ice cream, Hellmann's mayonnaise, Lawry's seasoned salt, Lipton ice tea, Ragú spaghetti sauce, and Wish-Bone salad dressings.

Mission Statement

The Junior League of Owensboro is an organization of women committed to promoting voluntarism, developing the potential of women, and improving the community through the effective action and leadership of trained volunteers. Its purpose is exclusively educational and charitable. The Junior League reaches out to women of all races, religions, and national origins who demonstrate an interest in and a commitment to voluntarism.

Contents

Contents

Current Projects

In an effort to support children and families in our community, the Junior League of Owensboro supported the following projects during the years of preparing this cookbook:

Court Appointed
Special Advocates

Grandma's Corner

Great Starts

Junior League
Art Garden

Owensboro Area
Museum of Science
and History

History

$\mathcal{A}$ member of the Association of Junior Leagues International, Inc., the Junior League of Owensboro was founded in 1974. Over three hundred women locally commit their time and talents to improve our community through volunteer service.

The women of the Junior League of Owensboro come from diverse backgrounds, with careers ranging from independent businesswomen to homemakers to corporate executives. These women express their common interest in voluntarism and a commitment to improving the quality of life for all who reside in Owensboro.

Because of this common interest, the Junior League trains women to be professionals in the volunteer community. The Junior League of Owensboro develops, researches, and undertakes projects in priority areas such as family and human services, health, education, and cultural enrichment.

In the world today, many negative influences surround our families, our friends, and our communities. On a daily basis, we read and hear about violent crime, drug abuse, teen pregnancy, poverty, and more. These issues grip our hearts and motivate us to do something about them in our community. This defines the Junior League of Owensboro—a desire, a belief, and an unwavering optimism that we can and do change things in our community.

How do we do this? The Junior League of Owensboro organizes annual fund-raising events to provide the financial means that sustain our community projects. Major sources of revenue and other resources for implementing our projects include: an annual charity ball, an annual rummage sale, cookbook sales, membership dues, and contributions.

Introduction

Owensboro, located on the Ohio River, is one of the largest cities in Kentucky. Originally known as "Yellowbanks," in reference to the color of the soil along the riverbanks, Owensboro was settled in 1797. Though the Owensboro area has grown steadily, its "small town quality" of a friendly city of warmhearted and hospitable people remains.

Since 1937, a group of women who formed what was originally known as the Cotillion Club has been working to ensure that Owensboro's children and families have a voice in the community. Today, the Junior League of Owensboro is over three hundred members strong and continues to meet many of the needs in our community through financial contributions and volunteer services.

This cookbook, *Home Again, Home Again*, a sequel to the Junior League of Owensboro's award-winning *To Market, To Market* cookbook, exemplifies Owensboro's hospitable attitude by sharing some of our best recipes from residents and hometown restaurants, plus some of the history of what makes Owensboro a special place to live. From our kitchen to yours, we present a collection of tasty recipes that will help you put together memorable meals to bring some of Owensboro's warmheartedness to your family table.

Home Again, Home Again's predecessor, *To Market, To Market,* served the Owensboro-Daviess County community well. The *Southern Living* Hall of Fame award-winning cookbook provided thousands of dollars that the Junior League of Owensboro donated to more than thirty agencies and groups during the past twenty years. The Junior League of Owensboro hopes that the proceeds from *Home Again, Home Again* will have the same lasting impact on children and families for many years to come.

Menus

Girls' Night Out

Wine Slush

Raspberry Brie in Rye

Pasta Peyton

Gruyère Grits Soufflé

Cream Cheese Muffin Puffs

Espresso Chocolate Mousse

Symphony Supper

Chilled Mocha Punch

Pesto Cherry Tomatoes

Lobster Bisque

Strawberry Spinach Salad

Grilled Boneless Lamb

Romaine Soufflé

Elegant Egg Braid

Buttery Italian Cream Cake

Derby Day Delights

Kentucky Mint Julep

Derby Party Mix

Broccoli Cauliflower Salad

Grilled Kentucky Bourbon Beef Tenderloin

Kentucky Corn Pudding

Bluegrass Blue Biscuits

Amazing Amaretto Cake

Holiday Feasts

Warm Cinnamon Punch

White Christmas Snack Mix

'Tis the Season Triple Layer Spread

Fabulous French Onion Soup

Grilled Beef Tenderloin with Mushrooms

Creamy Mashed Potatoes

Winter Vegetables with Mustard Sauce

Five-Day Coconut Cake

Menus

Garden Luncheon

Dazzling Lemonade Punch

Spring Garden Delight

Layered Tomato Salad

Summer Italian Chicken Pasta

Down East Blueberry Crescents

Ladyfinger Cheesecake

Melon Balls Melba

Spectacular Supper Club

Marvelous Margarita

Mango Bombay Spread

Blue Ribbon Salad

Chicken Parmesan with Spaghetti

Marinated Asparagus

Gougères

Ultimate Chocolate Sin Cake

Tailgating Treats

Kentucky's Hard Lemonade

Not Your Ordinary Sausage Balls

Dipity-Do-Da

Tangy Ham Rolls

Garlic Chicken Wings

Layered Pumpkin Bread

Oatmeal Crispies

Family Sunday Supper

Swinging on the Front Porch Tea

Early Harvest Salad

Country-Style Chicken Kiev

Marinated Vidalia Onions

Muenster Potatoes

Buttermilk Cloverleaf Rolls

Glazed Apple Pie

Very Vanilla Ice Cream

Home Again, Home Again

Home...Family...Tradition. Three small words that mean so much. One of the most important activities in a home is dining with family and friends. All special occasions are centered around food and socializing over the dinner table. Heavy traditions are evident when you recall holidays, birthdays, or just gatherings of family and friends. *Home Again, Home Again* is a collection of our favorite recipes, including some special guest chef appearances and a selection of recipes from our first award-winning cookbook, *To Market, To Market*.

Most memories begin and end in your family kitchen. Whether you are preparing Sunday dinner for all of your relatives or just discussing the school day with your children, you spend an enormous amount of time in the kitchen. We want you to treasure these recipes as much as we have and create your own memories as you do so. With everyone's busy schedules these days, it is nice to come home and have a relaxing dinner or just spend some time with your children enjoying our special Just for Kids section. Be thankful for these times with your family, and involve everyone in the process as you talk about your past and your future.

Tradition is visible within many homes. There may be a favorite dessert with dinner or a wonderful chocolate cake waiting for you when you arrive at your grandparents' home for a visit. *Home Again, Home Again* will provide the recipes for these traditions; you provide the memories. This will nourish your love for food and family. Our wish for *Home Again, Home Again* is that you will experience a strengthening of your traditions, your family, and your home and create memories that will last a lifetime as you prepare the wonderful recipes contained in this cookbook. So much time and love was put into the creation of this cookbook, and we are very proud to call it our own. We hope *Home Again, Home Again* will become a staple within your home for years to come. Enjoy!

Appetizers and Beverages

Appetizer Pie

8 ounces cream cheese, softened
2 tablespoons milk
1 (2-ounce) jar sliced dried beef, finely chopped
2 tablespoons dried minced onion
2 tablespoons finely chopped green bell pepper
1/2 teaspoon pepper
1/2 cup sour cream
1/2 cup chopped pecans

Beat the cream cheese and milk in a mixing bowl until creamy. Stir in the dried beef, onion, bell pepper and pepper. Add the sour cream and mix well.

Spoon the cream cheese mixture into an 8-inch baking dish and sprinkle with the pecans. Bake at 350 degrees for 15 minutes. Serve hot with assorted party crackers. SERVES 8 TO 10

Blue Cheese Fondue

16 ounces cream cheese, cubed
8 ounces blue cheese, crumbled
1/2 cup milk
1/2 cup (or more) dry white wine
1 teaspoon Worcestershire sauce
1/8 teaspoon salt

Combine the cream cheese, blue cheese, milk, wine, Worcestershire sauce and salt in a double boiler. Cook over medium to high heat until blended, adding additional wine as needed for the desired consistency and stirring frequently.

Transfer the cheese mixture to a fondue pot. Serve warm with fresh vegetable chunks and/or French bread cubes. SERVES 20

Raspberry Brie in Rye

2 (7-inch) round loaves rye bread
1 (15-ounce) round Brie cheese
1/2 cup seedless raspberry jam
1/4 cup sliced almonds

Slice 1/2 inch from the top of 1 bread loaf using a serrated knife and reserve the top. Place the Brie on top of the loaf and trace around the outer edge of the Brie with a knife. Remove the Brie and set aside. Using the traced mark as a guide, cut the loaf vertically 2 inches deep. Discard the bread, leaving a 2×5-inch shell.

Cut the rind from the top of the Brie and place the Brie in the bread shell. Spread the top of the Brie with the jam and sprinkle with the almonds. Arrange the loaf on a baking sheet. Bake at 325 degrees for 25 minutes or until the Brie is soft. Cut the remaining bread loaf and reserved top into 1-inch cubes. Serve warm with the bread cubes or assorted party crackers. SERVES 15

Dipity-Do-Da

2 cups sour cream
2 cups Hellmann's mayonnaise
8 ounces Cheddar cheese, finely shredded
Salt and pepper to taste
1 pound sliced bacon, crisp-cooked and crumbled
3 tomatoes, chopped

Combine the sour cream, mayonnaise and cheese in a bowl and mix well. Season with salt and pepper. Fold in the bacon and tomatoes. Chill, covered, for 3 hours.
MAKES 4 CUPS

NOTE: Serve with tortilla chips or spread on toasted sliced French bread.

Cheese Pâté

8 ounces cream cheese, softened
1 cup (4 ounces) grated Parmesan cheese
1/2 cup Hellmann's mayonnaise
3 green onions, chopped
2 tablespoons bacon bits
1 teaspoon parsley flakes
Cayenne pepper to taste

Beat the cream cheese in a mixing bowl until creamy. Stir in the Parmesan cheese, mayonnaise, green onions, bacon bits and parsley flakes.

Spread the cheese mixture in a round baking dish and sprinkle with cayenne pepper. Bake at 300 degrees for 15 to 20 minutes or until light brown and bubbly. Serve with assorted party crackers. SERVES 8 TO 10

Improving the lives of children and families in Owensboro is the goal of the Junior League of Owensboro. With a focus on children, we collect and distribute "Loving Layettes" to the neediest children born into the community. We provide education and training for parents needing basic child care skills. The Junior League of Owensboro started the Court Appointed Special Advocate program in Daviess County and continues to provide volunteer time and talent to that organization. The Junior League of Owensboro also supports Grandma's Corner, a crisis drop-off child care center. Since many members are mothers, we understand the stress and challenges parents endure and support a center where parents can take their children when they need a break.

DAVID MUNSTER,
AMERICAN BOUNTY
RESTAURANT

Homegrown means
something special to
David and Jenny
Munster, owners of
American Bounty
Restaurant. They use
locally produced food to
create their cuisine,
which changes with each
season depending on the
foods available in the
area. Celebrating special
occasions takes on new
meaning at this upscale
restaurant in downtown
Owensboro.

Baked Artichoke and Crab Meat Dip

1 package pita bread, split into rounds
Vegetable oil for deep-frying
4 (14-ounce) cans quartered artichoke hearts, drained
   and rinsed
1 cup Hellmann's mayonnaise
6 tablespoons freshly grated Parmesan cheese
8 ounces fresh jumbo lump crab meat, shells and
   cartilage removed
1/2 cup thinly sliced scallion tops
1 garlic clove, minced
1 tablespoon fresh lemon juice
1 teaspoon kosher salt
1/8 teaspoon cayenne pepper
2 tablespoons freshly grated Parmesan cheese
1 tablespoon chopped fresh parsley

Cut each round into quarters. Deep-fry the pita quarters
in hot oil in a deep-fat fryer until golden brown. Drain on
paper towels.

Beat the artichokes in a small mixing bowl using the
paddle attachment until of the consistency of a chunky
paste. Add the mayonnaise, 6 tablespoons cheese, crab
meat, scallion tops, garlic, lemon juice, kosher salt and
cayenne pepper and beat until the ingredients are evenly
incorporated but not smooth.

Spoon the artichoke mixture into a baking dish and
sprinkle with 2 tablespoons cheese. Bake at 400 degrees
until brown and bubbly. Sprinkle with the parsley. Serve
warm with the pita chips. SERVES 6 TO 8

NOTE: For a healthier option, bake the pita chips
instead of deep-frying. Arrange the pita quarters on a
baking sheet sprayed with nonstick cooking spray and
bake at 375 degrees until golden brown.

Hot Feta Artichoke Dip

1 (14-ounce) can artichoke hearts, drained and chopped
8 ounces feta cheese, crumbled
1 cup Hellmann's mayonnaise
1/2 cup (2 ounces) grated Parmesan cheese
1 (2-ounce) jar diced pimento, drained
1 garlic clove, minced

Combine the artichokes, feta cheese, mayonnaise, Parmesan cheese, pimento and garlic in a bowl and mix well. Spoon the artichoke mixture into a 3-cup baking dish.

Bake at 350 degrees for 20 to 30 minutes or until brown and bubbly. Garnish with sliced tomatoes and sliced green onions. Serve with assorted party crackers or pita wedges. SERVES 6 TO 8

Southern Shrimp Dip

32 ounces cream cheese, softened
1 pound cooked shrimp, peeled, deveined and chopped
1 tomato, chopped
1 onion, chopped
4 mild banana chiles, chopped
3 torrido or Santa Fe chiles, chopped
1 teaspoon garlic juice

Combine the cream cheese, shrimp, tomato, onion, banana chiles, torrido chiles and garlic juice in a saucepan. Cook over low to medium heat until heated through, stirring frequently; do not boil. Spoon the shrimp mixture into a chafing dish. Serve with scoop corn chips or baked pita points. SERVES 15 TO 20

Monterey Jack Salsa

Combine one drained 4-ounce can diced green chiles, one chopped drained 4-ounce can black olives, 1 chopped tomato, 4 chopped green onions, 1/4 cup chopped fresh cilantro, 1/2 cup Wish-Bone Italian salad dressing and 2 cups shredded Monterey Jack cheese in a bowl and mix well. Chill, covered, until serving time. Serve with assorted party crackers. Add additional salad dressing before serving, if desired, for a thinner consistency.

SERVES 8 TO 10

Fresh Asparagus Salsa

1/4 cup Bertolli olive oil
1/4 cup balsamic vinegar
2 teaspoons each chopped garlic, fresh basil, fresh thyme and parsley
2 cups chopped seeded peeled tomatoes
3 cups fresh asparagus tips, blanched and chopped
1/2 cup chopped sun-dried tomatoes
Salt to taste

Mix the olive oil, vinegar, garlic, basil, thyme and parsley in a bowl. Add the tomatoes, asparagus, sun-dried tomatoes and salt and toss to coat. Marinate, covered, in the refrigerator for 1 hour; drain. Serve with baked pita chips. You may prepare up to 2 days in advance and store, covered, in the refrigerator. SERVES 12

NOTE: This is so easy and refreshing for a spring appetizer. Try serving with a variety of chips for more pizzazz!

Mango Bombay Spread

8 ounces cream cheese, softened
4 ounces sharp Cheddar cheese, shredded
1/2 teaspoon curry powder
1/3 cup mango chutney
1/4 cup chopped pecans
2 tablespoons finely minced green onions
2 tablespoons dried currants, chopped

Combine the cream cheese, Cheddar cheese and curry powder in a bowl and mix well. Spread the cream cheese mixture on a round platter, forming a base. Spread the chutney over the prepared layer and sprinkle with the pecans, green onions and currants in the order listed. Chill, covered with plastic wrap, until serving time. Serve with Wheat Thins. SERVES 6

Spring Garden Delight

1 tablespoon unflavored gelatin
1/2 cup hot water
2 cups Hellmann's mayonnaise
1 onion, chopped and drained

2 cucumbers, chopped and drained
1 large green bell pepper, chopped
2 tomatoes, peeled, chopped and drained
Salt and pepper to taste

Dissolve the unflavored gelatin in the hot water. Combine with the mayonnaise in a bowl and mix well. Stir in the onion, cucumbers, bell pepper, tomatoes, salt and pepper. Spoon into a 1-quart glass serving bowl. Chill, covered, for several hours. Let stand at room temperature for 15 minutes. Serve with Triscuits. SERVES 25

'Tis the Season Triple Layer Spread

1 cup loosely packed coarsely chopped
   fresh spinach
1 cup loosely packed fresh basil
1 teaspoon minced garlic
1/4 cup Bertolli olive oil
1 cup (4 ounces) freshly grated
   Parmesan cheese

Salt and pepper to taste
8 ounces cream cheese, softened
4 ounces soft goat cheese, softened
1/4 cup finely chopped walnuts
1/4 cup finely chopped drained oil-pack
   sun-dried tomatoes

Line a 3-cup bowl with plastic wrap, allowing a 4-inch overhang. Brush the plastic wrap with vegetable oil. Process the spinach, basil and garlic in a food processor until finely chopped. Add the olive oil gradually, processing constantly until blended. Add the Parmesan cheese and process just until almost smooth. Season with salt and pepper.

Beat the cream cheese and goat cheese in a mixing bowl until smooth. Spread 1/3 of the cream cheese mixture over the bottom of the prepared bowl. Layer with 1/2 of the spinach mixture, 1/2 of the walnuts and 1/2 of the sun-dried tomatoes. Drop 1/2 of the remaining cream cheese mixture by spoonfuls over the prepared layers and spread evenly to the edge of the bowl. Repeat the process with the remaining spinach mixture, remaining walnuts, remaining sun-dried tomatoes and remaining cream cheese mixture in the order listed. Fold the plastic wrap over the top and press gently to compact. Chill for 8 to 10 hours or for up to 3 days.

To serve, unfold the plastic wrap on the top and invert the bowl onto a serving platter. Remove the bowl and plastic wrap. Let stand at room temperature for 30 minutes. Serve with assorted party crackers and/or party bread. SERVES 15

Derby Party Mix

2 (6-ounce) cans whole almonds
  (2¹/₄ cups)
1 (7-ounce) jar dry-roasted cashews
  (1¹/₃ cups)
1 (8-ounce) jar dry-roasted peanuts
1 (5-ounce) can chow mein noodles

6 tablespoons margarine or butter
1¹/₂ tablespoons Worcestershire sauce
1¹/₂ tablespoons soy sauce
3 dashes of hot sauce, or more
  to taste
1 (15-ounce) package raisins

Mix the almonds, cashews, peanuts and chow mein noodles in a large baking pan sprayed with nonstick cooking spray. Heat the margarine in a saucepan until melted. Stir in the Worcestershire sauce, soy sauce and hot sauce.

Drizzle the margarine mixture over the almond mixture and toss to coat. Bake at 325 degrees for 15 minutes, stirring occasionally. Let stand until cool. Stir in the raisins. Store in an airtight container for several weeks. SERVES 12

Pesto Cherry Tomatoes

1¹/₂ cups fresh basil
¹/₄ cup Bertolli olive oil
¹/₄ cup (1 ounce) grated Parmesan
  cheese
2 tablespoons pine nuts

2 garlic cloves
Salt to taste
1 pound cherry tomatoes
8 ounces mozzarella cheese, cut into
  ¹/₂-inch squares

Process the basil, olive oil, Parmesan cheese, pine nuts, garlic and salt in a food processor until puréed.

Cut the cherry tomatoes horizontally into halves. Scoop out the seeds and invert the halves onto paper towels. Drain for 30 minutes.

Fill each tomato half with pesto and level with a knife. Top ¹/₂ of the pesto-filled tomato halves with the cheese squares. Spear the rounded end of 1 cheese-topped tomato half with a wooden pick and push the wooden pick through the cheese square into the pesto-filled surface of another tomato half. Repeat the process with the remaining tomato halves. SERVES 20 TO 30

NOTE: If time is of the essence, substitute commercially prepared pesto for the homemade pesto.

Bacon Tomato Blossoms

10 to 15 canned refrigerator biscuits
8 slices bacon, crisp-cooked and chopped
1 large (or 2 small) tomato, chopped
3 ounces Swiss cheese, shredded
1/4 cup Hellmann's mayonnaise
1/4 small white onion, chopped
1 teaspoon basil

Separate each biscuit horizontally into 3 layers. Press each layer over the bottom and up the side of a miniature muffin cup. Combine the bacon, tomato, cheese, mayonnaise, onion and basil in a bowl and mix well.

Fill each prepared muffin cup 1/2 full with the bacon mixture. Bake at 375 degrees for 10 to 12 minutes or until brown and bubbly. You may prepare the filling 1 day in advance and store, covered, in the refrigerator. MAKES 30 TO 45 BLOSSOMS

Mexican Corn Dip

1 (24-ounce) can whole kernel corn, drained
6 cups (24 ounces) shredded Mexican cheese blend
1 (4-ounce) can diced green chiles, drained
1 cup Hellmann's mayonnaise
1 cup sour cream
3 green onions, chopped
1 jalapeño chile, chopped
1/2 teaspoon garlic salt

Mix the corn, cheese, green chiles, mayonnaise, sour cream, green onions, jalapeño chile, and garlic salt in a bowl. Chill, covered, for 4 to 10 hours; the flavor is enhanced if chilled overnight. Serve cold, or spoon into a 9×13-inch baking dish and bake at 325 degrees for 20 to 30 minutes or until heated through. Serve with tortilla chips.
SERVES 15 TO 25

Not Your Ordinary Sausage Balls

8 ounces fresh mushrooms, chopped
1 1/2 cups chopped celery
3/4 cup chopped green onions

1/2 teaspoon Lawry's seasoned salt
2 pounds sausage

Sauté the mushrooms, celery, green onions and seasoned salt in a skillet until the vegetables are tender. Remove from the heat. Roll or pat the sausage on a 6×10-inch cutting board. Cut the sausage into 20 squares.

Fill each sausage square with 1 tablespoon of the mushroom mixture and shape into a ball to enclose the filling. Arrange the balls on a baking sheet. Bake at 350 degrees for 10 to 15 minutes or until brown and crisp; drain. Serve immediately. You may freeze for future use, if desired. MAKES 20 SAUSAGE BALLS

Chicken and Ham Pinwheels

4 boneless skinless chicken breasts
8 thin slices cooked ham
4 teaspoons lemon juice
1/4 teaspoon paprika
1/4 teaspoon basil
1/4 teaspoon garlic powder

1/4 teaspoon salt
1/4 teaspoon pepper
1/4 cup Hellmann's mayonnaise
1 teaspoon dill weed
Sesame crackers and/or party rye slices

Pound the chicken 1/4 inch thick between sheets of waxed paper. Arrange 2 slices of ham on each chicken breast and roll to enclose the ham. Arrange the rolls seam side down in a baking dish. Drizzle with lemon juice and sprinkle with paprika, basil, garlic powder, salt and pepper.

Bake at 350 degrees for 40 minutes. Cool slightly and chill, covered, in the refrigerator. Cut each roll into 1/4-inch slices. Mix the mayonnaise and dill weed in a bowl.

To serve, layer the crackers and/or bread slices with 1 pinwheel and a dollop of the mayonnaise mixture. You may prepare in advance and store, covered, in the refrigerator for several days or freeze, tightly covered, for up to 3 months, topping with the mayonnaise mixture just before serving. SERVES 20

Coconut Chicken

3 pounds boneless skinless chicken breasts,
  $^1/_3$ to $^1/_2$ inch thick
2 teaspoons salt
2 teaspoons sugar
1 cup cornstarch
$^1/_4$ cup flour
2 cups flaked coconut
2 eggs
$^1/_4$ cup water
Vegetable oil
Red Plum Sauce (sidebar)

Cut the chicken into portions that measure 4 inches long and $^1/_2$ inch wide. Sprinkle the chicken with the salt and sugar and place in a resealable plastic bag; seal tightly. Marinate in the refrigerator for 4 hours. Rinse the chicken lightly and drain.

Combine the cornstarch, flour and coconut in a shallow dish and mix well. Whisk the eggs and water in a bowl until blended. Dip the chicken into the egg wash and coat with the coconut mixture.

Fry the chicken in hot oil in a skillet until light brown; drain. Serve with Red Plum Sauce. SERVES 6

Red Plum Sauce

Mix 1 cup red plum jam, 1 tablespoon prepared mustard, 1 tablespoon prepared horseradish and 1 teaspoon lemon juice in a saucepan. Cook over low heat until warm, stirring constantly.

MAKES 1 CUP

REID'S ORCHARD

Every October, Reid's Orchard Apple Festival celebrates the start of cool weather and the changing colors of the leaves with events that include a craft show, carnival, horse rides, corn maze, live music, and lots of food, including a wide variety of apple delicacies. More than 23,000 people attend this two-day event to sample food and drink. Reid's Hot Apple Cider (at right) is a festival favorite.

Reid's Hot Apple Cider

1¹/2 teaspoons whole allspice
1 teaspoon whole cloves
1 gallon Reid's apple cider
¹/2 cup packed brown sugar

6 (3-inch) cinnamon sticks
1 tablespoon (heaping) frozen orange juice concentrate

Tie the allspice and cloves in a coffee filter. Combine the cider and brown sugar in a stockpot and mix well. Add the allspice bag, cinnamon sticks and orange juice concentrate to the cider mixture.

Simmer over low heat for 20 minutes or until heated through, stirring occasionally; do not boil. Ladle the cider into mugs. You may store the cider in the refrigerator and reheat in the microwave as desired. Reid's apple cider may be purchased and frozen for future use. To freeze, drain 1 cup of the cider from the jar, replace the cap, and freeze. SERVES 20

Spiced Cranberry Cider

1 quart apple cider
3 (64-ounce) cans cranberry juice
3 tablespoons brown sugar

2 (3-inch) cinnamon sticks
³/4 teaspoon whole cloves
¹/2 lemon, thinly sliced

Bring the cider, cranberry juice and brown sugar to a boil in a saucepan, stirring occasionally. Tie the cinnamon sticks, cloves and lemon slices in a cheesecloth bag. Add the spice bag to the cider mixture. Simmer for 20 to 25 minutes. Discard the cheesecloth bag and ladle the cider into mugs. MAKES 30 (8-OUNCE) SERVINGS

Kentucky's Hard Lemonade

1 (12-ounce) can frozen lemonade concentrate or
  pink lemonade concentrate, thawed
2 (12-ounce) cans beer
1¹/₂ cups vodka

Mix the lemonade concentrate and beer in a large container. Add the vodka and mix well. Chill until serving time. Pour over ice in glasses. MAKES 2 QUARTS

Kentucky Mint Julep

SIMPLE SYRUP
¹/₄ cup sugar
2 tablespoons boiling water

MINT JULEP
3 or 4 fresh mint leaves
Crushed ice
1 ounce 100 proof Kentucky bourbon

For the syrup, combine the sugar and boiling water in a small heatproof bowl and stir until the sugar dissolves.

   For the mint julep, place 3 or 4 mint leaves in a julep glass and add crushed ice. Press down with a spoon to bruise the leaves. Add 1 ounce bourbon and 1 tablespoon of the Simple Syrup and mix well. Pack the glass with additional crushed ice and fill with additional bourbon. Garnish with additional mint leaves. SERVES 1

NOTE: Traditionally, this is served in a frosted silver mint julep cup.

Marvelous Margarita

1 cup tequila
1 (12-ounce) can frozen limeade
  concentrate

1 (12-ounce) can lemon-lime soda,
  chilled

Combine the tequila, limeade concentrate and soda in a blender and process until blended. Pour over ice in glasses. SERVES 4 TO 6

Warm Cinnamon Punch

1 (64-ounce) can pineapple juice
1 (64-ounce) can cranberry juice
2 cups water

1 cup packed light brown sugar
3 cinnamon sticks
1 tablespoon whole cloves

Combine the pineapple juice, cranberry juice and water in a large electric percolator. Place the brown sugar, cinnamon sticks and cloves in the percolator basket. Perk for 10 minutes or longer. Pour into mugs.

To prepare on the stovetop, combine the pineapple juice, cranberry juice, water, brown sugar, cinnamon sticks and cloves in a large saucepan and mix well. Simmer over low heat, stirring occasionally. Discard the cinnamon sticks and cloves and ladle into mugs. MAKES 30 (6-OUNCE) SERVINGS

Dazzling Lemonade Punch

1 1/4 cups water
1 cup sugar
1 1/4 cups fresh lemon juice

1 cup fresh raspberries
1 pint pineapple sherbet
3 cups carbonated water, chilled

Boil 1 1/4 cups water and the sugar in a small saucepan for 2 minutes or until the sugar dissolves, stirring occasionally. Let stand until cool. Combine the cooled syrup, lemon juice and raspberries in a large pitcher and mix gently. Chill, covered, for 2 hours. Scoop the sherbet into a punch bowl or pitcher. Stir the carbonated water into the raspberry mixture and pour over the sherbet. Ladle into punch cups. MAKES 2 QUARTS

Chilled Mocha Punch

1 1/2 quarts water
1/2 cup instant chocolate drink mix
1/2 cup sugar
1/2 cup instant coffee granules
1/2 gallon Breyers chocolate ice cream
1/2 gallon Breyers vanilla ice cream
1 cup whipped cream

Bring the water to a boil in a large saucepan. Remove from the heat. Add the drink mix, sugar and coffee granules to the boiling water and stir until dissolved. Chill, covered, for 8 to 10 hours.

Pour the coffee mixture into a punch bowl 30 minutes before serving. Scoop the ice cream into the punch bowl and top with dollops of whipped cream. Ladle into punch cups. SERVES 20

Top of the Morning Punch

2 quarts boiling water
2 cups sugar
2 ounces instant coffee granules
1 gallon Breyers vanilla ice cream
2 quarts milk
6 ounces Kahlúa (optional)

Combine the boiling water, sugar and coffee granules in a heatproof container and stir until dissolved. Chill, covered, for 8 to 10 hours.

To serve, place the ice cream in a punch bowl and let stand at room temperature for 30 minutes to soften. Add the milk, coffee mixture and liqueur to the punch bowl and stir gently. Ladle into punch cups. SERVES 18

NOTE: Great served at a breakfast gathering or brunch shower.

Swinging on the Front Porch Tea

6 cups water
1/2 cup Lipton instant peach tea
 granules

1 1/2 cups apricot nectar
3/4 cup ginger ale
1/2 cup white grape juice

Combine the water and tea granules in a pitcher and stir until the tea granules are dissolved. Stir in the apricot nectar, ginger ale and grape juice. Chill, covered, until serving time. Pour over ice in glasses. SERVES 10

Strawberry Shimmer

1 (10-ounce) package frozen
 strawberries in heavy syrup, thawed
2 cups cranberry juice, chilled

1 (750-milliliter) bottle Champagne,
 chilled

Process the undrained strawberries in a blender until puréed. Combine the puréed strawberries, cranberry juice and Champagne in a pitcher and mix well. Pour over ice in glasses. MAKES 6 CUPS

Wine Slush

2 liters burgundy
2 liters lemon-lime soda
1 cup sugar

1 (12-ounce) can each frozen cranberry
 juice concentrate, orange juice
 concentrate and lemonade concentrate

Combine the wine, soda, sugar, cranberry juice concentrate, orange juice concentrate and lemonade concentrate in a large freezer container and mix well. Freeze, covered, for 24 hours or longer.

 To serve, let the wine mixture stand at room temperature for 5 to 10 minutes. Stir until slushy and ladle into punch cups or goblets. SERVES 20 TO 24

Breads and Breakfast

 *Great Harvest Bread Co.® Croutons*

Great Harvest Dakota bread or any Great Harvest bread, sliced
Grace's Sunsational Seasonings toasted garlic bread dipping oil
Grated Parmesan cheese

Cut the bread slices into cubes. Spread the cubes in a single layer on a baking sheet and brush lightly with the dipping oil. Bake at 225 degrees for 2 hours for crunchy croutons. Decrease the baking time for softer croutons. Sprinkle with cheese.

Store in a jar with a tight-fitting lid in the refrigerator. The slow toasting of the bread ensures that the croutons will stay crunchy when tossed with salad greens and dressing. MAKES A VARIABLE AMOUNT

Bluegrass Blue Biscuits

¹/₂ cup (1 stick) butter
4 ounces blue cheese, crumbled
1 (10-count) can biscuits, cut into quarters

Heat the butter in a round baking dish until melted. Sprinkle the cheese over the butter. Arrange the biscuit quarters point side up in the prepared baking dish. Bake using the biscuit can directions. SERVES 10

AIMEE SANDERS-GARRARD, GREAT HARVEST BREAD CO.®, OWENSBORO

Aimee Sanders-Garrard, current owner of Great Harvest Bread Co.® in Owensboro and a member of the Junior League of Owensboro, offers this recipe. Aimee suggests preparing these croutons with the end of a loaf of Great Harvest bread. Any of the Great Harvest breads work wonderfully for this recipe, she says, but the nutty flavors of Dakota are brought out by toasting.

Kentucky Corn Bread

3 cups self-rising cornmeal
1/3 cup sugar
3 cups sour cream
1 1/2 cups vegetable oil
6 eggs, lightly beaten
2 2/3 cups cream-style corn
1/2 cup honey
1/4 cup (1/2 stick) butter, softened

Mix the cornmeal and sugar in a bowl. Stir in the sour cream, oil, eggs and corn. Spoon the batter into 2 greased and floured loaf pans. Bake at 350 degrees for 1 hour. Cool in the pan for 10 minutes. Invert onto a wire rack.

Mix the honey and butter in a bowl until blended. Slice the warm corn bread and serve with the honey butter. You may freeze for future use. MAKES 2 LOAVES

South-of-the-Border Corn Bread

1 pound hot bulk pork sausage
1 small onion, chopped
1 (4-ounce) can diced green chiles, drained
1 1/2 cups cornmeal
1 cup cream-style corn
1 cup sour cream
2 eggs, beaten
2 cups (8 ounces) shredded Cheddar cheese

Brown the sausage in a skillet, stirring until crumbly. Stir in the onion and green chiles. Cook for 5 minutes, stirring frequently; drain.

Combine the cornmeal, corn, sour cream and eggs in a bowl and mix well. Stir in the sausage mixture. Spoon 1/2 of the batter into a greased 9×13-inch baking pan and sprinkle with the cheese. Top with the remaining batter. Bake at 350 degrees for 30 minutes. Serve immediately. SERVES 12

Gougères

1 cup water
5 tablespoons butter
1 tablespoon salt
¼ teaspoon nutmeg
1 cup flour
1 cup (4 ounces) shredded Gruyère cheese
5 eggs, at room temperature
Nutmeg to taste

Bring the water, butter, salt and ¼ teaspoon nutmeg to a boil in a saucepan over medium-high heat. Boil until the butter melts, stirring occasionally; reduce the heat to low. Stir in the flour.

Cook until the mixture pulls from the side of the saucepan, stirring constantly with a wooden spoon. Remove from the heat. Add the cheese and stir until blended. Add 4 of the eggs 1 at a time, beating well after each addition. Beat until the mixture is shiny and smooth.

Drop the batter by spoonfuls onto a baking sheet. Bake at 425 degrees for 15 to 20 minutes, brushing the tops of the gougères with the remaining egg halfway through the baking process. Sprinkle with nutmeg to taste and serve.
MAKES 3 DOZEN GOUGÈRES

NOTE: These are excellent for pre-dinner wine tastings. They may be prepared several days in advance or frozen for up to one week.

Jalapeño Butter

Combine ½ cup softened butter, 1 minced garlic clove, 1 or 2 chopped seeded jalapeño chiles and 1 tablespoon chopped fresh cilantro in a bowl and mix well. Refrigerate, covered, for 8 hours or longer. Serve with hot rolls, corn bread, baked potatoes, rice or chicken.

MAKES ½ CUP

Cheese Popover Ring

1 cup water
1/2 cup (1 stick) butter
1 teaspoon salt
1/8 teaspoon pepper
1 cup flour
4 eggs, at room temperature
1 cup (4 ounces) finely chopped sharp Cheddar cheese or
  Gruyère cheese

Bring the water, butter, salt and pepper to a boil in a saucepan. Boil until the butter melts, stirring occasionally. Turn off the heat. Add the flour immediately and stir with a wooden spoon until the mixture pulls from the side of the saucepan. Remove the saucepan from the burner. Add the eggs 1 at a time, beating after each addition until the eggs are incorporated and the mixture is smooth and elastic.

Add the cheese to the flour mixture and mix well. Drop the dough by rounded tablespoonfuls around the outer edge of a greased round baking pan. If a round baking pan is not available, form a ring in the center of a baking sheet. Bake at 400 degrees for 35 to 45 minutes or until puffed and brown.

For variety, add 1/4 cup toasted almonds and 1/4 cup finely chopped green onions with the cheese. Sprinkle 1/4 cup almonds over the top of the ring before baking. Or, add 3 tablespoons mixed fresh herbs, such as parsley, dill weed and chives, with finely chopped Gruyère cheese or Swiss cheese. SERVES 15 TO 20

Elegant Egg Braid

8 cups flour
2 envelopes dry yeast
$^1/_3$ cup sugar
1 tablespoon salt
$^3/_4$ cup ($1^1/_2$ sticks) butter or margarine,
  cut into small chunks
2 cups warm (125-degree) milk
2 eggs, beaten
Vegetable oil
1 egg, beaten

Combine the flour, yeast, sugar and salt in a bowl and mix well. Cut in the butter with a pastry blender. Add the warm milk and 2 eggs and stir until combined. Knead the dough on a lightly floured work surface until all of the flour is incorporated. Knead for 10 minutes longer.

Preheat the oven to 200 degrees. Place the dough in a heatproof bowl and brush the top of the dough lightly with oil; cover with a clean tea towel. Turn off the oven. Place the bowl in the warm oven. Let stand with the door closed for 1 hour or until doubled in bulk. Punch the dough down and divide into 4 equal portions.

Roll each portion into an 18- to 24-inch rope. Braid loosely on a baking sheet and cover with a clean tea towel. Return the baking sheet to the warm oven. Let rise for 30 minutes or until doubled in bulk. Brush the top of the loaf with 1 beaten egg. Bake at 350 degrees for 20 minutes. SERVES 10 TO 12

NOTE: Wow your guests with this beautiful presentation!

Horseradish Butter

Combine $^1/_2$ cup softened butter, 8 ounces softened cream cheese, $^1/_4$ cup Hellmann's mayonnaise and $^1/_4$ cup drained horseradish in a mixing bowl and beat until fluffy. Store, covered, in the refrigerator. Bring to room temperature before serving.

MAKES 2 CUPS

Buttermilk Cloverleaf Rolls

1 envelope dry yeast
2 tablespoons warm water
3/4 cup buttermilk
1/4 cup vegetable oil
2 tablespoons sugar

1/2 teaspoon salt
2 1/4 cups flour
1/4 teaspoon baking soda
1/2 cup (1 stick) butter, melted

Dissolve the yeast in the warm water in a small bowl and stir. Heat the buttermilk, oil, sugar and salt in a saucepan over low heat until lukewarm, stirring occasionally. Remove from the heat. Stir in the yeast mixture.

Sift the flour and baking soda into a bowl and mix well. Stir in the buttermilk mixture. Let stand for 10 minutes.

Place 1 teaspoon of the butter in each of 12 muffin cups. Shape the dough by tablespoonfuls into balls and arrange 3 balls in each prepared muffin cup. Drizzle with the remaining butter. Let stand for 30 minutes. Bake at 425 degrees for 10 to 12 minutes or until light brown. Serve immediately. MAKES 1 DOZEN ROLLS

Dillseed Rolls

1 envelope dry yeast
1/2 cup warm water
1 cup creamed cottage cheese
1 tablespoon butter
1 egg, lightly beaten
2 tablespoons sugar

2 tablespoons dried minced onion
3 to 4 teaspoons dillseeds
1 teaspoon salt
1/4 teaspoon baking soda
2 1/2 cups plus 2 rounded tablespoons
   flour

Dissolve the yeast in the warm water and stir. Heat the cottage cheese in a saucepan until lukewarm, stirring occasionally. Add the butter to the cottage cheese and stir until melted. Remove from the heat. Stir in the yeast mixture, egg, sugar, onion, dillseeds, salt and baking soda. Add the flour gradually, beating constantly until a stiff dough forms.

Let rise, covered, for 50 to 60 minutes or until doubled in bulk; the dough will be sticky. Stir the dough and spoon into greased muffin cups. Let rise for 30 to 40 minutes or until doubled in bulk. Bake at 350 degrees for 20 minutes or until golden brown. Brush the tops of the warm rolls with additional melted butter and sprinkle lightly with additional salt. Freeze for future use, if desired. MAKES 1 1/2 DOZEN ROLLS

Anything Goes Bread

3 cups flour
1 teaspoon cinnamon
1 teaspoon salt
1 teaspoon baking soda
Nutmeg to taste
2 cups sugar

1 1/2 cups vegetable oil
3 eggs
1 teaspoon vanilla extract
1 (21-ounce) can cherry pie filling
1 cup chopped nuts

Mix the flour, cinnamon, salt, baking soda, nutmeg and sugar in a bowl. Add the oil, eggs, vanilla, pie filling and nuts and stir until combined. Spoon the batter into 2 greased and floured loaf pans or a greased and floured tube pan.

Bake at 350 degrees for 1 hour or until the loaves test done. Cool in the pans for 10 minutes. Remove to a wire rack. MAKES 2 LOAVES

NOTE: For variety, use different pie fillings.

Cranberry Pumpkin Bread

3 1/2 cups flour
1 1/2 cups sugar
2 teaspoons baking soda
2 teaspoons pumpkin pie spice
3/4 teaspoon salt
1 teaspoon baking powder
1 (16-ounce) can whole cranberry sauce

3/4 cup chopped pecans
2/3 cup vegetable oil
4 eggs, lightly beaten
1 cup confectioners' sugar
1/4 cup thawed frozen orange juice
  concentrate
1/8 teaspoon allspice

Mix the flour, sugar, baking soda, pie spice, salt and baking powder in a bowl. Combine the cranberry sauce, pecans, oil and eggs in a bowl and mix well. Add the cranberry mixture to the flour mixture and stir until combined. Spoon the batter into 2 greased 5×9-inch loaf pans. Bake at 325 degrees for 65 minutes or until a wooden pick inserted in the center of the loaves comes out clean. Cool in the pans for 10 minutes. Remove to a wire rack.

Combine the confectioners' sugar, orange juice concentrate and allspice in a bowl and mix well. Drizzle the glaze over the warm loaves and slice as desired. MAKES 2 LOAVES

Mocha Nut Bread

2 cups flour
1 cup sugar
1/2 cup baking cocoa
1/4 cup instant coffee granules
1/2 teaspoon baking soda
1/4 teaspoon salt

1 1/4 cups sour cream
1/3 cup butter, melted
2 eggs, lightly beaten
1 cup (6 ounces) chocolate chips
1/2 cup chopped walnuts (optional)

Combine the flour, sugar, baking cocoa, coffee granules, baking soda and salt in a bowl and mix well. Mix the sour cream, butter and eggs in a bowl. Stir the flour mixture into the sour cream mixture. Fold in the chocolate chips and walnuts.

Spoon the batter into a greased and floured 5×9-inch loaf pan. Bake at 350 degrees for 50 to 55 minutes or until the top appears glazed and the edges pull from the sides of the pan. Cool in the pan for 10 minutes. Remove to a wire rack. Freezes well.
MAKES 1 LOAF

Poppy Seed Bread

BREAD
3 cups flour
2 cups sugar
1 1/2 teaspoons salt
1 1/2 teaspoons baking powder
1 1/2 cups milk

1 cup plus 2 tablespoons vegetable oil
3 eggs
1 1/2 tablespoons poppy seeds
1 1/2 teaspoons each almond extract,
    vanilla extract and butter extract

ORANGE FROSTING
3/4 cup sugar
1/4 cup orange juice

1/2 teaspoon each almond extract,
    vanilla extract and butter extract

For the bread, combine the flour, sugar, salt, baking powder, milk, oil, eggs, poppy seeds and flavorings in a mixing bowl. Beat at medium speed for 2 minutes, scraping the bowl occasionally. Spoon the batter into 6 lightly greased miniature loaf pans. Bake at 350 degrees for 45 minutes. Cool in the pans for 5 minutes.

For the frosting, combine the sugar, orange juice and flavorings in a bowl and mix well. Drizzle over the warm loaves. Let stand in the pans for 5 minutes longer. Remove the loaves to a wire rack. MAKES 6 MINIATURE LOAVES

Layered Pumpkin Bread

BREAD

3 1/3 cups flour

4 teaspoons pumpkin
 pie spice

2 teaspoons baking soda

1 teaspoon baking
 powder

1 1/2 teaspoons salt

2 2/3 cups sugar

2/3 cup vegetable oil

4 eggs

1 (16-ounce) can pumpkin

2/3 cup water

CREAM CHEESE FILLING

16 ounces cream cheese,
 softened

3/4 cup sugar

2 eggs

1 teaspoon vanilla extract

BROWN SUGAR TOPPING

2 tablespoons brown
 sugar

2 tablespoons flour

1 tablespoon butter,
 melted

1 teaspoon cinnamon

1/4 teaspoon pumpkin
 pie spice

For the bread, sift the flour, pie spice, baking soda, baking powder and salt into a bowl and mix well. Beat the sugar and oil in a mixing bowl until light and fluffy. Beat in the eggs 1 at a time. Beat in the pumpkin. Add the flour mixture to the pumpkin mixture alternately with the water, beating well after each addition.

For the filling, beat the cream cheese in a mixing bowl until creamy. Add the sugar, eggs and vanilla and beat until blended.

For the topping, combine the brown sugar, flour, butter, cinnamon and pie spice in a bowl and stir until crumbly.

Spoon 1/4 of the batter into each of 2 greased 5×9-inch loaf pans. Spread each layer with 1/2 of the filling and top with the remaining batter. Sprinkle with the topping. Bake at 350 degrees for 45 to 60 minutes or until a wooden pick inserted in the center comes out clean. Cool in the pans for 10 minutes. Remove to a wire rack. MAKES 2 LOAVES

WeatherBerry Muffin Kabobs

Prepare and bake your favorite muffins in miniature muffin cups. Each kabob requires 3 muffins, all one flavor or three different flavors. It was a tradition at WeatherBerry to use pecan, banana and pumpkin muffins. Cut 6-inch doilies into halves and fold accordion style. You will need 2 doily accordions for each muffin kabob. To assemble 1 kabob, thread 1 accordion doily first, 3 muffins and another accordion doily onto a cellophane-frilled wooden pick. The accordion doilies may be threaded first and toward the center of the kabob or as desired by the hostess. The muffin kabobs are typically placed in the upper left-hand corner of the plate.

Fruit Streusel Coffee Cake

1 (2-layer) package yellow cake mix
1 cup flour
1 envelope dry yeast
2/3 cup warm water
2 eggs
1 (21-ounce) can cherry pie filling or
   other fruit pie filling

1/3 cup butter or margarine
1 cup confectioners' sugar
1 tablespoon light corn syrup
1 tablespoon water

Combine 1 1/2 cups of the cake mix, the flour and yeast in a bowl and mix well. Add the warm water and stir until blended. Add the eggs and mix well. Spoon the batter into a greased 9×13-inch baking pan. Spread the pie filling over the top.

   Mix the butter and remaining cake mix in a bowl until crumbly and sprinkle over the prepared layers. Bake at 350 degrees for 25 to 30 minutes or until the edges pull from the sides of the pan.

   Mix the confectioners' sugar, corn syrup and 1 tablespoon water in a bowl. Drizzle over the warm coffee cake. Slice and serve warm. SERVES 15

NOTE: May be prepared in muffins cups or individual coffee cake pans.

Graham Streusel Cake

2 cups graham cracker crumbs
3/4 cup chopped nuts
3/4 cup packed brown sugar
3/4 cup (1 1/2 sticks) butter, melted
1 1/4 teaspoons cinnamon
1 (2-layer) package yellow cake mix

1 cup water
1/4 cup vegetable oil
3 eggs
1 cup confectioners' sugar
2 tablespoons milk

Mix the graham cracker crumbs, nuts, brown sugar, butter and cinnamon in a bowl.

   Combine the cake mix, water, oil and eggs in a bowl and mix well. Layer the batter and crumb mixture 1/2 at a time in a greased and floured 9×13-inch baking pan, ending with the crumb mixture. Bake at 350 degrees for 35 minutes. Cool in the pan on a wire rack. Mix the confectioners' sugar and milk in a bowl. Drizzle over the cooled cake. SERVES 15

Mocha-Glazed Coffee Cake

MOCHA FILLING
6 tablespoons sugar
3 tablespoons cinnamon

2 tablespoons instant coffee granules
2 tablespoons baking cocoa

COFFEE CAKE
2 cups flour
1 teaspoon baking powder
1/2 teaspoon salt
2 cups sugar

1 cup (2 sticks) butter, softened
2 eggs
1/2 teaspoon vanilla extract
1 cup sour cream

MOCHA FROSTING AND ASSEMBLY
1 teaspoon instant coffee granules
1 tablespoon hot water
4 ounces cream cheese, softened
6 tablespoons butter, softened
*1/2 cup plus 2 tablespoons sifted
   confectioners' sugar*

1/2 teaspoon vanilla extract
1/2 teaspoon orange juice
Chopped walnuts

For the filling, combine the sugar, cinnamon, coffee granules and baking cocoa in a bowl and mix well.

For the coffee cake, sift the flour, baking powder and salt into a bowl and mix well. Beat the sugar and butter in a mixing bowl until creamy. Beat in the eggs until blended. Stir in the vanilla. Add the flour mixture alternately with the sour cream, beating well after each addition.

Spoon 1/2 of the batter into a greased and floured bundt pan and sprinkle with the filling. Top with the remaining batter. Bake at 350 degrees for 50 to 60 minutes or until the coffee cake tests done. Cool in the pan for 20 minutes. Invert onto a serving platter.

For the frosting, dissolve the coffee granules in the hot water in a small bowl. Let stand until cool. Beat the cream cheese and butter in a mixing bowl until light and fluffy. Add the confectioners' sugar gradually, beating constantly until blended. Beat in the vanilla, orange juice and coffee mixture. Beat for 4 minutes longer or until doubled in bulk. Spread the frosting over the top and side of the cake and sprinkle with walnuts. Chill, covered, until serving time. SERVES 16

Butterscotch Breakfast Bars

1 cup chopped pecans
3/4 cup packed brown sugar
1/2 cup (1 stick) butter
1 (4-ounce) package butterscotch cook-and-serve or
    instant pudding mix
1/2 teaspoon cinnamon
24 frozen dinner yeast rolls

Spray the bottom and side of a bundt pan with nonstick cooking spray. Sprinkle the pecans over the bottom of the prepared pan. Heat the brown sugar and butter in a saucepan until blended, stirring frequently. Stir in the pudding mix and cinnamon.

   Arrange the frozen rolls in the prepared pan and pour the brown sugar mixture over the rolls. Let rise at room temperature for 8 to 10 hours. Bake at 350 degrees for 35 to 40 minutes or until brown and bubbly. Invert onto a serving platter and serve immediately. SERVES 16

Down East Blueberry Crescents

8 ounces cream cheese, softened
1 cup (2 sticks) margarine, softened
2 cups flour
Blueberry jelly or any flavor jelly
Confectioners' sugar

Beat the cream cheese, margarine and flour in a mixing bowl until blended. Divide the cream cheese mixture into 2 equal portions. Wrap each portion in waxed paper. Chill for 8 to 10 hours.

   Roll each portion 1/8 inch thick on a lightly floured work surface; cut with a biscuit cutter. Spoon 1 scant teaspoon jelly onto each round. Fold over and pinch the edges to seal. Arrange the crescents on a baking sheet. Bake at 350 degrees for 20 minutes. Sprinkle immediately with confectioners' sugar. MAKES 1 TO 1 1/2 DOZEN CRESCENTS

Top of the Morning Danish

16 ounces cream cheese, softened
1 cup sugar
1 egg yolk
1 teaspoon vanilla extract
2 (8-count) cans crescent rolls

2 cups confectioners' sugar
1/2 teaspoon vanilla extract
1/2 cup (more or less) milk
Fresh blueberries

Beat the cream cheese, sugar, egg yolk and 1 teaspoon vanilla in a mixing bowl until creamy, scraping the bowl occasionally. Unroll the crescent roll dough of 1 can. Pat the dough over the bottom of a greased 9×13-inch baking pan, pressing the edges and perforations to seal. Spread with the cream cheese mixture.

Unroll the dough of the remaining can and press over the prepared layers, pressing the edges and perforations to seal. Bake at 350 degrees for 25 to 35 minutes or until brown.

Mix the confectioners' sugar, 1/2 teaspoon vanilla and milk in a bowl until the desired consistency. Drizzle the glaze over the baked layer and sprinkle with blueberries. Store, covered, in the refrigerator. Reheat individual servings, if desired. Substitute cinnamon or cherry pie filling for the blueberries for variety. SERVES 15

ABC Muffins

2 cups shredded apples
1 1/3 cups sugar
1 cup frozen blueberries
1 cup shredded carrots
1 cup chopped pecans
2 1/2 cups flour

1 tablespoon baking powder
2 teaspoons baking soda
2 teaspoons cinnamon
1/2 teaspoon salt
1/2 cup vegetable oil
2 eggs, lightly beaten

Combine the apples and sugar in a large bowl and mix well. Fold in the blueberries, carrots and pecans. Mix the flour, baking powder, baking soda, cinnamon and salt in a bowl. Add the flour mixture to the apple mixture and stir just until moistened. Whisk the oil and eggs in a bowl until blended. Add the egg mixture to the apple mixture and stir just until combined. Fill greased or paper-lined muffin cups 2/3 full. Bake at 375 degrees for 20 to 25 minutes or until the muffins test done. Cool in the pans for 5 minutes. Remove to a wire rack. Freeze for future use, if desired.
MAKES 1 1/2 DOZEN MUFFINS

Baklava Muffins

FILLING

1/2 cup chopped walnuts

1/3 cup sugar

3 tablespoons butter, melted

1 1/2 teaspoons cinnamon

MUFFINS AND ASSEMBLY

1 cup plus 7 tablespoons flour

1/4 cup sugar

2 teaspoons baking powder

1/2 teaspoon baking soda

1 cup plus 2 tablespoons buttermilk

3 tablespoons unsalted butter, melted

1 egg

1/2 cup honey

For the filling, mix the walnuts, sugar, butter and cinnamon in a bowl.

For the muffins, mix the flour, sugar, baking powder and baking soda in a bowl. Whisk the buttermilk, butter and egg in a large measuring cup until blended. Make a well in the center of the flour mixture and pour the buttermilk mixture into the well. Stir just until moistened. Overmixing will produce tough muffins. Line 12 muffin cups with paper liners. Fill the prepared muffin cups 1/3 full and sprinkle with a scant tablespoon of the filling. Add enough of the remaining batter to each muffin cup to fill 2/3 full. Sprinkle with the remaining filling.

Bake at 400 degrees for 15 minutes or until golden brown. Remove the muffins to a wire rack and drizzle with the honey. Heating the honey will make the drizzling process easier. You may substitute a mixture of 3/4 cup plain yogurt and 1/3 cup low-fat milk for the buttermilk. Freeze for future use, if desired. MAKES 1 DOZEN MUFFINS

Butter Melt Muffins

2 cups self-rising flour

1 cup sour cream

1 cup (2 sticks) unsalted butter or margarine, melted

Combine the flour, sour cream and butter in a bowl and stir just until moistened. Fill lightly greased miniature muffin cups full. Bake at 350 degrees for 25 minutes or until light brown. MAKES 2 1/2 DOZEN MINIATURE MUFFINS

Cream Cheese Muffin Puffs

1/2 cup sugar
1 teaspoon cinnamon
1/8 teaspoon almond extract
1/4 cup (1/2 stick) butter, melted
1/2 teaspoon vanilla extract
1 (10-count) can buttermilk biscuits
3 ounces cream cheese, cut into 10 cubes

Mix the sugar, cinnamon and almond extract in a bowl. Mix the butter and vanilla in a bowl. Separate the dough into 10 biscuits. Press or roll each biscuit into a 3-inch circle.

Dip each cream cheese cube into the butter mixture and coat with the sugar mixture. Arrange 1 cube in the center of each circle and fold the dough over the cube to cover. Shape into a ball to seal. Dip each ball into the butter mixture and coat with the sugar mixture.

Arrange seam side down in ungreased muffin cups. Bake at 375 degrees for 12 to 18 minutes or until golden brown. Store, covered, in the refrigerator. MAKES 10 PUFFS

Praline Muffins

1 cup packed brown sugar
1 cup pecans, chopped
1/2 cup flour
2/3 cup butter, melted
2 eggs, beaten

Combine the brown sugar, pecans and flour in a bowl and mix well. Whisk the butter and eggs in a bowl until blended. Add the butter mixture to the brown sugar mixture and stir just until moistened.

Fill greased miniature muffin cups 2/3 full. Bake at 350 degrees for 15 minutes. Cool in the pans for 5 minutes. Remove to a wire rack. MAKES 3 DOZEN MINIATURE MUFFINS

Raspberry Muffins

1/4 cup flour
1/4 cup finely chopped pecans
1/4 cup packed brown sugar
2 tablespoons butter, softened
1 1/2 cups flour
1/2 cup sugar

2 teaspoons baking powder
1/2 cup milk
1/2 cup (1 stick) butter, melted
1 egg, lightly beaten
1 1/2 cups frozen raspberries

Combine 1/4 cup flour, the pecans, brown sugar and 2 tablespoons butter in a bowl and stir until crumbly.

Mix 1 1/2 cups flour, the sugar and baking powder in a bowl. Add the milk, 1/2 cup butter and egg and stir just until moistened. Fold in the raspberries. Fill greased muffin cups 2/3 full. Sprinkle with the pecan mixture and pat lightly. Bake at 375 degrees for 20 to 25 minutes or until the muffins test done. Cool in the pan for 5 minutes. Remove to a wire rack. Freeze for future use, if desired. MAKES 1 DOZEN MUFFINS

Cinnamon Pecan Scones

1/2 cup (1 stick) butter or margarine,
  softened
2/3 cup cinnamon chips
2 tablespoons heavy cream
4 cups baking mix

1 cup cinnamon chips
1 cup chopped pecans
1/4 cup sugar
1 1/2 cups heavy cream

Beat the butter at medium speed in a mixing bowl until creamy. Combine 2/3 cup cinnamon chips and 2 tablespoons cream in a microwave-safe bowl. Microwave on High for 1 minute, stirring once. Stir until blended. Let stand until cool. Add to the butter and mix well. Store, covered, in the refrigerator. Serve at room temperature.

Combine the baking mix, 1 cup cinnamon chips, pecans and sugar in a bowl and mix well. Make a well in the center of the baking mix mixture. Add 1 1/2 cups cream to the well and stir just until moistened.

Pat the dough 3/4 inch thick on a sheet of waxed paper. Cut with a 2 1/2-inch round biscuit cutter. Arrange the rounds in a 9×13-inch baking pan. Repeat the process with the dough scraps. Bake at 400 degrees for 15 to 20 minutes or until light brown. Remove to a serving platter immediately. Serve the scones with the cinnamon butter. MAKES 14 SCONES

Savory Sausage Bread

1 pound hot bulk pork sausage, crumbled
1 pound mild bulk pork sausage, crumbled
1/2 cup chopped onion
1 tablespoon butter
3 cups baking mix or white cornmeal
1 cup milk
1/3 cup Hellmann's mayonnaise
1/2 cup (2 ounces) grated Parmesan cheese
1/2 cup (2 ounces) shredded Swiss cheese
2 eggs, beaten
1 teaspoon water
1 egg

Brown the sausage in a skillet; drain. Sauté the onion in the butter in a skillet until tender; drain. Combine the baking mix, milk, mayonnaise, Parmesan cheese, Swiss cheese and 2 beaten eggs in a bowl and mix well.

Spread 1/2 of the dough in a greased 9×13-inch baking pan. Sprinkle with the sausage and sautéed onion and top with the remaining dough. Whisk the water and 1 egg in a bowl until blended. Brush the top with the egg wash. Bake at 375 degrees for 30 minutes. Cut into squares and serve warm. SERVES 15

Sausage Gravy

Brown 1 pound bulk pork sausage in a skillet, stirring until crumbly. Drain, reserving 1/4 cup of the pan drippings. Mix 1/3 cup flour with the reserved pan drippings until smooth. Stir in the sausage, 2 1/4 cups half-and-half, 3/4 teaspoon salt and 1/2 teaspoon pepper. Cook over medium heat until thickened and bubbly, stirring frequently.

SERVES 6 TO 8

Sausage Rolls

2 loaves frozen bread dough, thawed
1 pound ground hot bulk pork sausage
1 cup finely chopped onion
$^1/_2$ cup finely chopped green bell pepper
$^1/_2$ cup finely chopped celery
1$^1/_2$ cups (6 ounces) shredded sharp Cheddar cheese
Butter, melted

Roll each bread loaf into a rectangle on a baking sheet. Brown the sausage in a skillet, stirring until crumbly; drain. Sprinkle the sausage, onion, bell pepper, celery and cheese evenly over the dough. Roll lengthwise to enclose the filling. Brush with melted butter.

Arrange the rolls seam side down on a baking sheet. Bake at 350 degrees for 30 to 40 minutes or until golden brown. Slice and serve warm. SERVES 20 TO 25

NOTE: Prepare 1 day in advance, wrap in greased foil and store in the refrigerator. Remove from the refrigerator and arrange the rolls seam side down on a baking sheet. Let stand at room temperature for 30 minutes. Bake as directed above.

Swiss Chalet Loaf

1 loaf French bread
1 (8-ounce) package sliced Swiss cheese
2 tablespoons chopped onion
1 tablespoon dry mustard
1 tablespoon poppy seeds
1 teaspoon Lawry's seasoned salt
$^1/_2$ cup (1 stick) margarine, melted

Make diagonal slits to but not through the loaf using a serrated knife. Arrange the loaf on a baking sheet lined with foil. Place 1 slice of cheese in each slit.

Mix the onion, dry mustard, poppy seeds, seasoned salt and margarine in a bowl. Drizzle the margarine mixture over the top of the loaf. Bake at 350 degrees for 40 minutes. Serve warm. SERVES 6 TO 8

Breakaway Vegetable Bread

8 ounces bacon, crisp-cooked and crumbled
1 cup (4 ounces) shredded Cheddar cheese
$^1/_2$ cup (2 ounces) grated Parmesan cheese
1 small onion, finely chopped
1 small green bell pepper, finely chopped
3 (10-count) cans buttermilk biscuits, cut into quarters
$^1/_2$ cup (1 stick) butter, melted

Combine the bacon, Cheddar cheese, Parmesan cheese, onion and bell pepper in a bowl
and mix well. Dip $^1/_3$ of the biscuit quarters into the butter and arrange in a bundt pan.
Sprinkle with $^1/_2$ of the bacon mixture. Dip $^1/_2$ of the remaining biscuit quarters into
the remaining butter and arrange over the prepared layers. Sprinkle with the remaining
bacon mixture. Dip the remaining biscuit quarters into the remaining butter and
arrange over the top. Bake at 350 degrees for 40 to 45 minutes or until light brown.
SERVES 16

Baked Grand Marnier French Toast

1 loaf French bread, cut into 1-inch slices
8 eggs
$2^1/_2$ cups milk
2 tablespoons Grand Marnier
1 tablespoon sugar
$^1/_2$ teaspoon vanilla extract
$^1/_2$ teaspoon salt
2 tablespoons butter, cut into small pieces
Confectioners' sugar

Arrange the bread slices in a single layer in a greased 9×13-inch baking pan. Whisk the
eggs, milk, liqueur, sugar, vanilla and salt in a bowl until blended. Pour the egg mixture
over the bread. Chill, covered, for 8 to 10 hours.

Remove the cover and dot with the butter. Bake at 350 degrees for 45 to 50 minutes
or until light brown and puffy. Sprinkle with confectioners' sugar and serve with syrup
and fresh fruit. SERVES 6

Honey Oat Bran Pancakes

1 (7-ounce) package honey bran muffin mix
3/4 cup milk
1/2 cup chopped pecans
1 small green or yellow apple, grated
2 egg whites
2 tablespoons brown sugar

Combine the muffin mix, milk, pecans, apple, egg whites and brown sugar in a bowl and mix well. Pour enough of the batter onto a hot nonstick griddle to make a 4-inch circle. Cook until golden brown on both sides, turning once. Repeat the process with the remaining batter. SERVES 4 TO 5

Vanilla Pecan Waffles

2¹/2 cups flour
2 tablespoons sugar
1 tablespoon plus 1 teaspoon baking powder
3/4 teaspoon salt
2¹/2 cups milk
3/4 cup vegetable oil
3/4 to 1 cup vanilla custard-style yogurt
1/2 cup chopped pecans (optional)
2 eggs, beaten
1 teaspoon vanilla extract

Combine the flour, sugar, baking powder and salt in a bowl and mix well. Add the milk, oil, yogurt, pecans, eggs and vanilla to the flour mixture and whisk just until moistened.

Cook in a waffle iron sprayed with nonstick cooking spray using the manufacturer's directions. You may freeze for future use and reheat in a toaster. SERVES 4

Bird's Nest Eggs

12 thin slices Canadian bacon
12 ounces Swiss cheese, shredded
12 eggs
1 cup heavy cream
Salt and pepper to taste
1/3 cup grated Parmesan cheese
1 teaspoon paprika
1/4 cup chopped fresh parsley
6 English muffins, split and heated

Arrange the bacon in a single layer in a lightly greased 9×13-inch baking dish. Sprinkle each slice with some of the Swiss cheese, making a nest over each slice of bacon. Chill, covered, in the refrigerator. Break 1 egg in the center of each cheese nest. Pour the cream over the top and sprinkle with salt and pepper.

Bake at 425 degrees for 10 minutes. Sprinkle with the Parmesan cheese and paprika. Bake for 8 to 10 minutes longer or until set. Sprinkle with the parsley. Let stand for 10 minutes. Cut into 12 equal portions and serve on the warm muffins halves. SERVES 12

Eggs Olé

1/2 cup flour
1 teaspoon baking powder
1 teaspoon salt
10 eggs
2 cups cottage cheese
2 (4-ounce) cans diced green chiles
1/2 cup (1 stick) butter, melted
16 ounces Monterey Jack cheese, shredded

Mix the flour, baking powder and salt together. Whisk the eggs in a bowl until blended. Stir in the flour mixture, cottage cheese, green chiles and butter. Fold in the Monterey Jack cheese. Pour the egg mixture into a greased 9×13-inch baking pan. Bake at 350 degrees for 45 minutes or until set. Serve with salsa. SERVES 8 TO 10

Bluegrass Breakfast Pie

2 cups milk
3 eggs
1/2 teaspoon spicy mustard
1/8 teaspoon paprika
1/8 teaspoon garlic powder
2 cups (8 ounces) shredded
  Cheddar cheese

1 1/2 cups chopped cooked country ham
4 slices white bread, torn
1/2 cup chopped onion
4 slices bacon, crisp-cooked, drained
  and crumbled
2 tablespoons chopped fresh parsley

Combine the milk, eggs, spicy mustard, paprika and garlic powder in a mixing bowl. Beat at medium speed for 1 minute or until blended. Stir in the cheese, ham, bread, onion, bacon and parsley.

    Pour the egg mixture into a greased 9×13-inch baking dish. Bake at 375 degrees for 30 minutes. Let stand for 10 minutes before serving. SERVES 8

Good Morning Pizza

1 teaspoon shortening
1 pound bulk pork sausage
1 (6-ounce) package pizza dough mix
1 cup frozen hash brown potatoes,
  thawed
1 cup (4 ounces) shredded
  Cheddar cheese

4 eggs
3 tablespoons milk
1/2 teaspoon salt
1/8 teaspoon pepper
2 tablespoons grated Parmesan cheese

Coat the bottom and side of a 12- or 14-inch pizza pan with the shortening. Brown the sausage in a skillet, stirring until crumbly; drain. Prepare the pizza dough using the package directions. Pat the dough over the bottom and up the side of the prepared pizza pan. Bake at 375 degrees for 2 to 3 minutes. Maintain the oven temperature.

    Sprinkle the sausage, hash brown potatoes and Cheddar cheese over the baked layer in the order given. Whisk the eggs, milk, salt and pepper in a bowl until blended and pour over the prepared layers. Sprinkle with the Parmesan cheese. Bake for 30 minutes or until brown and bubbly. Cut into wedges. SERVES 8

Spicy-and-Sour Quiche

1 unbaked (9-inch) pie shell
8 ounces spicy bulk pork sausage
$^1/_2$ cup chopped onion
$^3/_4$ cup shredded peeled tart apple
1 tablespoon lemon juice
1 tablespoon sugar
$^1/_8$ teaspoon red pepper flakes
1 cup (4 ounces) shredded Cheddar cheese
1$^1/_2$ cups half-and-half
3 eggs
$^1/_4$ teaspoon salt
$^1/_8$ teaspoon ground black pepper

Pierce the bottom and side of the pie shell with a fork and line with foil. Bake at 425 degrees for 10 minutes; discard the foil. Bake for 5 minutes longer or until light brown. Let stand until cool. Reduce the oven temperature to 375 degrees.

Brown the sausage with the onion in a skillet, stirring until the sausage is crumbly and the onion is tender; drain. Stir in the apple, lemon juice, sugar and red pepper flakes. Cook over medium-high heat for 4 minutes or just until the apple is tender and the liquid has evaporated, stirring frequently. Let stand until cool.

Spoon the sausage mixture into the pie shell and sprinkle with the cheese. Whisk the half-and-half, eggs, salt and black pepper in a bowl until blended. Pour the egg mixture over the sausage mixture. Bake for 35 to 45 minutes or until a knife inserted in the center comes out clean. Let stand for 10 minutes before serving. SERVES 6 TO 8

Sausage Grits

1 pound mild or hot bulk pork
  sausage
3 cups hot cooked grits
2 cups (8 ounces) shredded Cheddar
  cheese or any mixture of cheeses

3 tablespoons butter
1/8 teaspoon garlic salt
1/8 teaspoon pepper
1 1/4 cups milk
3 eggs

Brown the sausage in a skillet, stirring until crumbly; drain. Combine the hot grits, cheese, butter, garlic salt and pepper in a bowl and stir until the cheese and butter melt. Whisk the milk and eggs in a bowl until blended. Add the milk mixture to the grits mixture and mix well. Spoon the sausage into a greased 9×13-inch baking dish. Spread the grits mixture over the top. Bake at 350 degrees for 45 minutes or until set. Garnish with sliced tomatoes. SERVES 8

NOTE: This dish may be prepared in advance and refrigerated, covered, overnight. Let sit at room temperature for 15 minutes before baking.

Strawberry Patch Freezer Jam

1 quart fresh ripe strawberries
1/2 cup undrained canned crushed
  pineapple in heavy syrup
2 tablespoons lemon juice

5 cups sugar
3/4 cup water
1 (1 3/4-ounce) package Sure-Jel

Gently mash the strawberries in a bowl. Drain, reserving a small amount of the juice. The strawberry pulp and reserved juice should measure 2 cups. Add the pineapple, lemon juice and sugar to the strawberry pulp and mix well. Let stand for 20 minutes.
  Bring the water and Sure-Jel to a boil in a saucepan. Boil for 1 minute, stirring constantly. Add the Sure-Jel to the strawberry mixture and stir for 3 minutes. Ladle the jam immediately into sterilized jars with tight-fitting lids, leaving 1/4 inch headspace. Let stand at room temperature for 8 to 10 hours. Freeze until needed. MAKES 6 1/4 CUPS

Soups, Salads and Sandwiches

Chicken Velvet Soup

2 cups milk
1 cup heavy cream
6 cups chicken stock
3/4 cup (1 1/2 sticks) butter
3/4 cup flour
2 cups chopped cooked chicken
1 teaspoon Dijon mustard
1 teaspoon salt
1 teaspoon white pepper

Heat the milk, cream and stock in a saucepan. Melt the butter in a saucepan. Stir in the flour. Cook over medium heat for 2 minutes, stirring constantly. Stir in the milk mixture a small amount at a time. Cook until the mixture comes to a boil and is smooth and thickened, stirring constantly. Stir in the chicken, Dijon mustard, salt and white pepper. Cook until heated through. Ladle into soup bowls. Garnish with chopped fresh parsley.
SERVES 8

COLBY'S FINE FOOD & SPIRITS

Colby's Fine Food & Spirits has long been a fixture in the downtown restaurant scene of Owensboro. Their approach to quality and service invites customers to feel at home in the open, airy dining area and bar decorated with photographs of Owensboro's history.

Best-Ever White Chili

4 chicken breasts
5 cups chicken broth
2 chicken bouillon cubes
1 cup chopped onion
1 (4-ounce) can chopped green chiles
4 (15-ounce) cans Great Northern beans
1 cup salsa
2 garlic cloves, minced
1 tablespoon plus 1 teaspoon cumin
2 teaspoons oregano
2 teaspoons parsley flakes
1 teaspoon crushed red pepper
Salt and black pepper to taste

Combine the chicken, broth and bouillon cubes in a large saucepan. Cook until the chicken is cooked through and no longer pink. Remove the chicken from the broth to cool, reserving the broth in the saucepan. Tear the chicken into pieces.

Bring the reserved broth, onion and green chiles to a boil. Add the chicken pieces and beans and stir to mix well. Stir in the salsa. Add the garlic, cumin, oregano, parsley flakes, red pepper, salt and black pepper. Simmer over low heat for 30 minutes, stirring frequently to prevent sticking. Ladle into soup bowls. Garnish with sour cream, shredded Monterey Jack cheese, additional salsa and tortilla chips. SERVES 4

Lobster Bisque

3 tablespoons minced gingerroot
1 small onion, minced
3 tablespoons butter
4 cups (1 quart) lobster stock or chicken stock
1/2 cup white wine
1/4 cup cooking sherry
4 cups (1 quart) heavy cream
2 cups chopped partially cooked lobster meat
1 teaspoon Worcestershire sauce
Salt and pepper to taste

Sauté the gingerroot and onion in the butter in a large saucepan until the onion is soft. (Do not fry or brown.) Add the stock. Bring to a boil. Cook over medium-high heat for 10 to 15 minutes or until the liquid is reduced by 1/2. Add the white wine and sherry. Cook at a medium boil for 1 to 2 minutes. Add the cream, lobster meat, Worcestershire sauce, salt and pepper. Simmer for 10 to 15 minutes. Ladle into soup bowls. SERVES 4

NOTE: You may store, covered, in the refrigerator for 1 to 2 days.

Cooking lobster is easy when you follow these simple steps. To cook two 1- to 1^{1}/2-pound lobsters, fill a large kettle with 32 cups (8 quarts) salted water and bring to a boil. Place the lobsters in the water head first. Return the water to a boil and reduce the heat. Simmer for 20 minutes. Remove from the heat. Let the lobsters cool in the cooking liquid. Remove the cooled lobsters from the liquid. For each lobster, remove the tail by twisting the tail and body in opposite directions. Cut away the membrane from the tail to expose the meat using kitchen shears. Discard the vein that runs through the tail. Twist off the large claws where they join the body. Serve and enjoy.

Black-eyed peas are also called cow peas. Originating in Asia, the black-eyed pea is said to have been introduced to the United States through African slaves on Southern plantations. According to one American tradition in the south, eating black-eyed peas on New Year's Day brings a year of good luck and prosperity. Tradition also says this dish is to be served after every window and door in your home is opened (to let out any leftover bad luck) and a "lucky person" walks over the threshold, setting the tone for the new year. Try this Hoppin' John recipe (at right) for a year of good luck!

Hoppin' John Soup

1 pound bulk pork
  sausage
3 (15-ounce) cans black-
  eyed peas
2 cups chopped onions
1 cup finely chopped
  green bell pepper
1 chicken bouillon cube
1 tablespoon Lawry's
  seasoned salt
1/2 teaspoon pepper
1 or 2 dashes of Tabasco
  sauce
2 cups water
2 cups cooked white rice

Brown the sausage in a skillet, stirring until crumbly; drain. Combine the sausage and next 8 ingredients in a slow cooker and stir to mix well. Cook on Low for 6 to 8 hours or on High for 4 hours or longer to enhance the flavor. Spoon 1/3 cup cooked rice into each soup bowl. Ladle the soup over the rice. SERVES 6

Hearty Lentil Soup

1 cup lentils, sorted
1 cup water
1 garlic clove, minced
2 ribs celery, sliced
1/2 cup chopped onion
1 tablespoon butter
1 1/2 to 2 cups coarsely
  chopped potatoes
1 cup grated carrots
6 cups chicken broth
1 cup tomato juice
1 teaspoon salt
1 teaspoon thyme
1/3 cup uncooked brown
  rice
1 1/2 cups frozen corn

Rinse the lentils. Place the lentils and water in a bowl. Sauté the garlic, celery and onion in the butter in a large stockpot until tender. Stir in the potatoes and carrots. Drain the lentils and add to the vegetables. Add the next 5 ingredients. Bring to a boil and reduce the heat. Simmer, covered, for 30 minutes or until the lentils and potatoes are tender. Stir in the corn. Cook for 10 to 20 minutes longer. Ladle into soup bowls. SERVES 10

Fabulous French Onion Soup

SOUP

1/4 cup (1/2 stick) butter

2 tablespoons Bertolli olive oil

6 yellow onions, sliced

4 garlic cloves, minced

1 teaspoon sugar

1/3 cup Cognac

1 tablespoon Dijon mustard

1/2 teaspoon thyme

3 tablespoons flour

2 (10-ounce) cans beef broth

4 (10-ounce) cans beef consommé

1 cup dry white wine

CROUTONS

8 thick slices French bread

Butter to taste

Garlic powder and pepper to taste

ASSEMBLY

8 slices Gruyère cheese or Swiss cheese

For the soup, heat the butter and olive oil in a large stockpot until the butter melts. Add the onions. Cook over medium heat for 10 minutes, stirring occasionally. Add the garlic and sugar. Cook until the onions are translucent and tender. Add the Cognac, Dijon mustard and thyme. Stir in the flour. Cook for 3 minutes, stirring constantly. Stir in the broth, consommé and wine gradually. Simmer, uncovered, over medium-low heat for about 1 hour.

For the croutons, spread the bread with butter and sprinkle with garlic powder and pepper. Place on a baking sheet. Bake at 350 degrees until golden brown.

To assemble and serve, ladle the soup into microwave-safe bowls. Float a crouton in the center of each bowl. Top each with a slice of the cheese. Microwave on High until the cheese melts. SERVES 8

Baked Potato Soup

4 large baking potatoes, baked and
   cooled
2/3 cup margarine
2/3 cup flour
7 cups milk
4 green onions, sliced
12 slices bacon, crisp-cooked and
   crumbled

1¹/2 cups (6 ounces) shredded
   Cheddar cheese
1 cup sour cream
3/4 teaspoon salt
1/2 teaspoon pepper

Peel the potatoes and chop into pieces. Melt the margarine in a large stockpot. Stir in the flour until smooth. Add the milk gradually, stirring constantly. Cook until thickened, stirring constantly. Add the potatoes and green onions. Reduce the heat and simmer for 10 to 15 minutes. Add the bacon, cheese, sour cream, salt and pepper. Heat until the cheese melts, stirring constantly. Ladle into soup bowls. SERVES 8

Quick Tortellini and Spinach Soup

8 ounces fresh spinach, rinsed and
   drained
2 tablespoons Bertolli olive oil
2 ounces pancetta, finely chopped
3 garlic cloves, minced
1 onion, finely chopped
9 cups chicken broth or chicken stock

2 teaspoons Italian herb blend
   seasoning
9 ounces spinach or cheese tortellini
1 (28-ounce) can crushed tomatoes
Salt and pepper to taste
1 cup (4 ounces) freshly grated
   Parmesan cheese

Trim the spinach and coarsely chop. Heat the olive oil in a large stockpot over medium-high heat. Add the pancetta, garlic and onion. Cook for 10 to 15 minutes or until light brown, stirring frequently. Add the broth and Italian seasoning. Bring to a boil. Stir in the tortellini. Simmer, uncovered, for 10 to 12 minutes or until the tortellini is al dente. Stir in the tomatoes. Simmer for 5 minutes. Add the spinach. Cook for 3 minutes or just until the spinach is wilted. Season with salt and pepper. Ladle into soup bowls. Sprinkle with the cheese. SERVES 6 TO 8

NOTE: You may substitute Canadian bacon or ham for the pancetta.

Banana Salad

DRESSING
1 egg yolk, beaten
$1/2$ cup sugar
2 tablespoons vinegar
$1/2$ cup mayonnaise-type salad dressing

SALAD
12 bananas
1 cup crushed peanuts

For the dressing, combine the egg yolk, sugar and vinegar in a saucepan and mix well. Bring to a boil, stirring constantly to prevent sticking. Remove from the heat. Add the mayonnaise-type salad dressing gradually. Beat with a wire whisk until smooth.

For the salad, slice 2 or 3 of the bananas into a shallow bowl. Cover with a light layer of the dressing. Sprinkle with a layer of peanuts. Repeat the layers until all of the ingredients are used. SERVES 10 TO 12

MOONLITE
BAR-B-Q INN

The Bosley Family has been cooking up famous barbecue at the Moonlite Bar-B-Q Inn for nearly forty years and has incorporated many of their own family recipes into the menu. One recipe that dates back four generations is the Banana Salad—served daily on the Moonlite Buffet.

71

Apple Walnut Salad

1/4 cup vegetable oil
3 1/2 tablespoons lemon juice
1 garlic clove, minced
1/2 teaspoon sugar
1 teaspoon (about) yellow or brown
  mustard

1/2 teaspoon oregano
1 or 2 apples, cored and sliced
8 ounces sliced mushrooms
2 cups romaine
Walnut pieces to taste

Blend the oil, lemon juice, garlic, sugar, mustard and oregano in a medium mixing bowl. Add the apples and mushrooms and toss to mix well. Marinate in the refrigerator for 1 hour. Place the romaine in a salad bowl. Pour the apple mixture over the romaine. Sprinkle with walnut pieces. Garnish with crumbled blue cheese. SERVES 4

Mixed Salad Greens and Pears with Basil Vinaigrette

2 or 3 garlic cloves, chopped
1/2 cup sugar
3/4 cup chopped fresh basil
1/2 teaspoon salt
1/2 teaspoon pepper
1/2 cup cider vinegar

1 cup vegetable oil
3 pears
12 ounces mixed salad greens
1/2 cup dried cranberries
2/3 cup pecans, toasted and chopped
8 ounces Gorgonzola cheese, crumbled

Process the garlic, sugar, basil, salt and pepper in a blender until the basil is finely chopped. Add the vinegar and oil in a fine stream, processing constantly until blended.

Cut the pears into halves and discard the cores. Cut into thin slices. Combine the salad greens, pears, cranberries and pecans in a salad bowl. Pour the desired amount of vinaigrette over the salad and toss to coat. Sprinkle with the cheese. SERVES 12

NOTE: You may use canned pears if desired.

Romaine Orange Almond Salad

DRESSING
1/2 cup vegetable oil
1/4 cup vinegar
2 tablespoons sugar
2 tablespoons parsley
1 teaspoon salt
Dash of pepper

SALAD
1/4 cup sliced almonds
1 1/2 tablespoons sugar
1/2 head leaf lettuce, torn
1/2 head romaine, torn
1/2 cup chopped celery
4 green onions, sliced
1 (11-ounce) can mandarin oranges, drained

For the dressing, combine the oil, vinegar, sugar, parsley, salt and pepper in a container with a lid. Cover and shake well. Chill for 1 hour or longer.

For the salad, sauté the almonds and sugar in a skillet over low heat until the sugar is melted and the almonds are coated and brown. Remove from the heat to cool. Combine the leaf lettuce, romaine, celery and green onions in a salad bowl. Chill, covered, until ready to serve.

To serve, pour the dressing over the lettuce mixture. Add the mandarin oranges and toss to mix well. Sprinkle with the almonds. SERVES 6

Blue Ribbon Salad

SWEET-AND-SPICY PECANS

1/4 cup sugar

1 cup warm water

1 cup pecan halves

2 tablespoons sugar

1 tablespoon chili powder

1/8 teaspoon red pepper

BALSAMIC VINAIGRETTE

1/2 cup balsamic vinegar

3 tablespoons Dijon mustard

3 tablespoons honey

2 garlic cloves, minced

2 small shallots, minced

1/4 teaspoon salt

1/4 teaspoon pepper

1 cup Bertolli olive oil

SALAD

12 ounces mixed salad greens

4 ounces blue cheese, crumbled

2 oranges, thinly sliced

1 pint fresh strawberries, cut into
   quarters

For the pecans, dissolve 1/4 cup sugar in the warm water in a bowl. Add the pecans. Soak for 10 minutes; drain. Mix 2 tablespoons sugar, the chili powder and red pepper in a bowl. Add the pecans and toss to coat. Spread the pecans in a single layer on a baking sheet. Bake at 350 degrees for 10 minutes, stirring once.

For the vinaigrette, whisk the vinegar, Dijon mustard, honey, garlic, shallots, salt and pepper in a bowl until blended. Whisk in the olive oil gradually.

For the salad, combine the salad greens and cheese in a salad bowl. Add the vinaigrette and toss to coat. Divide among 6 salad plates. Arrange the orange slices over the salad greens. Sprinkle with the strawberries. Top with the pecans. SERVES 6

Strawberry Spinach Salad

1/4 cup apple cider vinegar
1/2 cup corn oil
1 1/2 teaspoons minced onion
2 tablespoons sesame seeds
1 tablespoon poppy seeds
1/2 cup sugar
1/4 teaspoon Worcestershire sauce

1/4 teaspoon paprika
1 (10-ounce) package fresh spinach, trimmed
1 pint fresh strawberries, sliced
8 ounces feta cheese, crumbled
1/2 cup chopped pecans

Combine the vinegar, corn oil, onion, sesame seeds, poppy seeds, sugar, Worcestershire sauce and paprika in a jar with a tight-fitting lid. Seal the jar and shake well.

Rinse the spinach and pat dry. Tear into bite-size pieces into a salad bowl. Add the strawberries, cheese and pecans. Pour the dressing over the salad and toss to coat.
SERVES 10

Greek Salad with Lemon Dill Dressing

LEMON DILL DRESSING
1/4 cup fresh lemon juice
1 tablespoon water
2 teaspoons red wine vinegar
5 ounces (10 tablespoons) vegetable oil

1/2 teaspoon dill weed
1/4 teaspoon garlic powder
2 tablespoons grated Parmesan cheese
Salt and pepper to taste

SALAD
2 cups torn lettuce (about 1/2 head)
4 tomatoes, seeded and chopped
1 large cucumber, thinly sliced
1/4 cup sliced pitted black olives
4 ounces feta cheese, crumbled

3 green onions, finely sliced
2 anchovies, mashed
2 tablespoons chopped parsley
Salt and freshly ground pepper to taste

For the dressing, combine the lemon juice, water, vinegar, oil, dill weed, garlic powder, cheese, salt and pepper in a jar with a tight-fitting lid. Seal the jar and shake to mix well.

For the salad, combine the lettuce, tomatoes, cucumber, olives, cheese, green onions, anchovies, parsley, salt and pepper in a large salad bowl and toss to mix. Pour the dressing over the salad and toss to coat. SERVES 6

Angel Hair Pasta Salad

2 pounds angel hair pasta
2 1/2 tablespoons Lawry's seasoned salt
1/2 cup lemon juice
1/2 cup plus 2 tablespoons vegetable oil
2 1/2 cups chopped celery
1 1/4 cups chopped green bell peppers
1 1/4 cups chopped onion

1 1/2 cups pitted black olives, chopped
2 (7-ounce) cans pimentos, drained
3 cups Hellmann's mayonnaise
2 cups diced tomatoes
1/4 cup (1 ounce) grated Parmesan
  cheese

Boil the pasta in water to cover in a saucepan for 5 minutes; drain. Rinse with cold water; drain. Mix the seasoned salt, lemon juice and oil in a large bowl. Add the pasta and toss to coat. Chill, covered, for 8 to 12 hours.

Add the celery, bell peppers, onion, olives, pimentos and mayonnaise to the chilled pasta mixture and toss to mix well. Chill, covered, for 1 hour or until ready to serve.

To serve, add the tomatoes to the pasta mixture and toss to mix. Sprinkle with the cheese. SERVES 8

Antipasto Magnifico

1 (8-ounce) bottle Wish-Bone Italian
  dressing
1 (6-ounce) jar pitted black olives,
  drained
1 (14-ounce) can artichoke hearts,
  drained and quartered
12 ounces cherry tomatoes,
  cut into halves

1 (8-ounce) package pepperoni
1 (8-ounce) package sliced salami, cut
  into strips
1 (12-ounce) jar pepperoncini, drained
8 ounces mushrooms
8 ounces Monterey Jack cheese,
  cut into cubes

Combine the dressing, olives, artichokes, cherry tomatoes, pepperoni, salami, pepperoncini and mushrooms in a 1-gallon resealable plastic bag. Marinate in the refrigerator for 8 to 12 hours, turning occasionally; drain, discarding the marinade. Add the cheese to the mixture in the bag and shake to mix. Serve over a bed of lettuce. SERVES 8

Sensational Salad

1 head iceberg lettuce,
  rinsed and drained
3 large tomatoes,
  cut into pieces
1 small onion, thinly
  sliced into crescent
  shapes
1 green bell pepper,
  cut into strips

1 tablespoon dried mint,
  or 1/2 cup chopped
  fresh mint
1 teaspoon garlic powder
1 teaspoon pepper
1/2 cup Bertolli olive oil
1/3 cup lemon juice
2 teaspoons salt

Tear the lettuce into bite-size pieces and place in a salad bowl. Add the tomatoes, onion, bell pepper and mint. Sprinkle with the garlic powder and pepper and toss to mix. Chill, covered, until ready to serve.

To serve, blend the olive oil, lemon juice and salt in a bowl. Pour over the salad mixture and toss to coat. Serve immediately. SERVES 8

Broccoli Cauliflower Salad

1 head cauliflower, cut
  into bite-size pieces
1 head broccoli, cut into
  bite-size pieces
1 cup cider vinegar
1 tablespoon sugar

1 tablespoon dill weed
1 tablespoon Lawry's
  seasoned salt
1 teaspoon each pepper,
  salt and garlic salt
1 1/2 cups vegetable oil

Combine the cauliflower and broccoli in a large bowl. Mix the vinegar, sugar, dill weed, seasoned salt, pepper, salt and garlic salt in a small bowl. Add the oil and blend well. Pour over the vegetables and toss to coat. Marinate, covered, in the refrigerator for 24 hours, stirring occasionally. You may add sliced carrots, if desired. SERVES 20

Early Harvest Salad

Break 1 head cauliflower into bite-size pieces. Trim 1 bunch green onions and 1/2 package radishes. Chop the green onions and radishes. Drain one 6-ounce can water chestnuts and chop. Combine the cauliflower, green onions, radishes, water chestnuts, 3/4 cup sour cream, 3/4 cup Hellmann's mayonnaise and 1 envelope buttermilk ranch salad dressing mix in a large bowl and toss to mix well. Chill, covered, for 2 hours before serving.

SERVES 8

Fresh Tomato Dressing

Whisk 1 cup Bertolli olive oil, $1/2$ cup balsamic vinegar, 3 sliced garlic cloves, 1 tablespoon sugar, 1 tablespoon salt and 1 tablespoon pepper in a large glass bowl. Stir in 4 chopped large tomatoes and 2 tablespoons fresh thyme leaves or 4 sprigs of fresh thyme. Let stand, covered, at room temperature for 1 hour, stirring occasionally. Chill, covered, for 8 hours.

MAKES 4 CUPS

Layered Tomato Salad

8 ounces fresh mozzarella cheese, cut into 8 slices
3/4 cup Fresh Tomato Dressing (sidebar)
3 large tomatoes, cut into 4 slices each
1 teaspoon salt
1 teaspoon pepper
24 fresh basil leaves

Arrange the cheese in a single layer in a shallow dish. Pour Fresh Tomato Dressing over the cheese. Chill, covered, for 1 hour. Remove the cheese, reserving the dressing.

Sprinkle the tomato slices evenly with salt and pepper. Place 1 tomato slice on each of 4 salad plates. Layer each with 1 cheese slice and 2 basil leaves, shredded. Repeat to form 4 stacks. Top each stack with a tomato slice and 2 basil leaves, shredded. Drizzle evenly with the reserved dressing. SERVES 4

NOTE: The dressing can be stored in the refrigerator for up to 1 month. Stir additional chopped fresh tomato into the dressing after each use.

Chicken Waldorf Salad

1¼ cups chicken stock
1 cup quick-cooking brown rice
1 red apple, chopped
1 tablespoon lemon juice
2 cups chopped cooked chicken breasts

1 cup seedless red or green grape halves
½ cup chopped celery
¼ cup raisins
½ cup Hellmann's mayonnaise
½ cup yogurt

Bring the stock to a boil in a 2-quart saucepan over medium heat. Add the rice. Cook, covered, over medium-low heat for 10 minutes or until all of the stock has been absorbed. Fluff the rice with a fork. Spread in an even layer on a large tray. Place in the freezer or in the refrigerator for 10 minutes to cool. Toss the apple with the lemon juice in a large bowl. Add the chicken, grapes, celery and raisins and toss to mix. Add the rice and toss to mix. Stir in the mayonnaise and yogurt. SERVES 6

Avocado Cheese Melt

2 large tomatoes, each cut into 4 slices
¼ teaspoon salt
¼ teaspoon pepper
1 large avocado, cut into 8 slices
1 tablespoon rice vinegar
¼ cup (½ stick) butter, softened
1 teaspoon grated Parmesan cheese
2 tablespoons Hellmann's mayonnaise

8 slices sourdough bread
4 ounces sharp Cheddar cheese, sliced
8 slices bacon, crisp-cooked and drained
4 ounces Monterey Jack cheese with
   peppers, sliced
4 ounces white Cheddar cheese, sliced
¼ cup Wish-Bone Thousand Island
   dressing

Sprinkle the tomatoes evenly with the salt and pepper. Sprinkle the avocado with the vinegar. Beat the butter and Parmesan cheese in a bowl until smooth.

Spread the mayonnaise on 1 side of 4 bread slices. Layer with 1 sharp Cheddar cheese slice, 1 tomato slice, 2 avocado slices, 2 bacon slices, 1 Monterey Jack cheese slice, 1 tomato slice and 1 white Cheddar cheese slice. Spread 1 side of the remaining bread slices with the dressing and place dressing side down on each sandwich.

Spread ½ of the butter mixture on 1 side of each sandwich. Cook 2 sandwiches at a time buttered side down in a hot nonstick skillet or on a griddle over medium heat for 2 to 3 minutes or until golden brown. Spread the remaining butter mixture evenly on the uncooked side of the sandwiches and turn. Cook for 2 to 3 minutes or until golden brown. MAKES 4 SANDWICHES

Tangy Ham Rolls

3 pounds thinly sliced deli ham
2 cups apple juice
2/3 cup packed brown sugar
1/2 cup sweet pickle relish
2 teaspoons prepared mustard
1 teaspoon paprika
12 Kaiser rolls, split

Separate the ham slices and place in a slow cooker. Combine the apple juice, brown sugar, relish, mustard and paprika in a small bowl and mix well. Pour over the ham. Cook, covered, on Low for 4 to 5 hours or until heated through. Place 3 or 4 slices of the ham on the bottom half of each roll. Top with the remaining halves. Serve with additional relish, if desired. SERVES 12

Pork Loin Sandwiches with Apple Jelly Sauce

1 (2 1/2-pound) boneless pork loin
1/4 cup canola oil
1 cup apple jelly
1 cup ketchup
2 teaspoons vinegar
1 1/2 teaspoons chili powder
1/2 teaspoon salt
1 teaspoon pepper
8 sandwich buns

Brown the pork in the canola oil in a skillet on all sides. Place in a pressure cooker. Cook according to the pressure cooker directions for 15 to 20 minutes or until cooked through. Shred the pork and place in a slow cooker. Combine the jelly, ketchup, vinegar, chili powder, salt and pepper in a bowl and mix well. Pour over the pork. Cook on Low for 2 hours to allow the pork to soak up the mixture. Serve warm on the buns.
SERVES 8

Side Dishes

Marinated Asparagus

1 pound fresh asparagus, trimmed
$^1/_2$ cup sugar
$^1/_2$ cup white vinegar
$^1/_4$ cup water
3 whole cloves
1 cinnamon stick
$1^1/_2$ teaspoons celery seeds
$^1/_2$ teaspoon salt

Steam the asparagus in a steamer until tender-crisp. Bring the sugar, vinegar, water, cloves, cinnamon stick, celery seeds and salt to a boil in a medium saucepan. Remove the cloves and cinnamon stick. Pour the mixture over the asparagus in a bowl. Marinate, covered, in the refrigerator for at least 2 to 3 hours before serving. SERVES 6 TO 8

Broccoli Parmesan

1 (16-ounce) package broccoli florets
2 tablespoons margarine
3 tablespoons chopped onion
2 tablespoons flour
1 teaspoon chicken bouillon granules
$1^3/_4$ cups milk
$^1/_2$ cup (2 ounces) grated Parmesan cheese
$^1/_2$ teaspoon salt
$^1/_2$ teaspoon pepper
$^1/_2$ teaspoon dry mustard
$^1/_4$ teaspoon marjoram

Steam the broccoli in a steamer for 5 minutes or until tender-crisp. Place in a serving bowl and keep warm. Melt the margarine in a saucepan. Add the onion. Sauté until the onion is tender. Stir in the flour and bouillon granules. Cook for 1 minute. Add the milk gradually, stirring constantly. Cook over medium heat until thickened and bubbly, stirring constantly. Stir in the cheese, salt, pepper, dry mustard and marjoram. Pour over the warm broccoli. SERVES 4 TO 6

Carrot Casserole

1 pound carrots, peeled and chopped
3 eggs, lightly beaten
1/2 cup sugar
1/2 cup (1 stick) butter or margarine, melted
3 tablespoons flour
1 teaspoon baking powder
1 teaspoon vanilla extract

Place the carrots in a saucepan and cover with water. Bring to a boil. Cook for 45 minutes or until the carrots are tender; drain. Process the carrots in a food processor until smooth. Combine the puréed carrots, eggs, sugar, butter, flour, baking powder and vanilla in a bowl and mix well. Spoon into a lightly greased 1-quart baking dish. Bake at 350 degrees for 45 minutes or until set. SERVES 8

Cheesy Corn Bake

2 tablespoons butter
2 tablespoons flour
1/2 teaspoon salt
1/4 teaspoon pepper
1/4 teaspoon hot sauce
1/2 cup milk
1/2 cup sour cream
2 cups fresh yellow corn
1/2 cup (2 ounces) shredded Swiss cheese
3 slices white bread
2 tablespoons butter, melted

Melt 2 tablespoons butter in a saucepan. Add the flour, salt, pepper and hot sauce. Stir in the milk and sour cream. Cook over low heat until thickened, stirring constantly. Stir in the corn and cheese. Spoon into a greased 1-quart baking dish.

Crumble the bread into a bowl. Add 2 tablespoons melted butter and toss to coat evenly. Sprinkle on top of the corn mixture. Bake at 350 degrees for 30 minutes or until brown and bubbly. SERVES 4

Kentucky Corn Pudding

$1/4$ cup sugar
3 tablespoons flour
2 teaspoons baking powder
2 teaspoons salt
6 eggs
2 cups heavy cream
$1/2$ cup (1 stick) butter or margarine, melted
6 cups fresh or frozen corn

Mix the sugar, flour, baking powder and salt together. Beat the eggs with a fork in a large bowl. Stir in the cream and butter. Add the sugar mixture gradually, stirring constantly. Stir in the corn. Pour into a lightly greased 9×13-inch baking dish. Bake at 350 degrees for 45 minutes or until deep golden brown and set. Let stand for 5 minutes before serving. SERVES 8

Dreamy Green Beans

2 tablespoons butter, melted
2 tablespoons flour
1 teaspoon sugar
1 teaspoon salt
$1/4$ teaspoon pepper
1 teaspoon grated onion
1 cup sour cream
2 (12-ounce) packages frozen French-style green beans, cooked and drained
8 ounces Cheddar cheese, shredded
$1/2$ cup cornflake crumbs
1 tablespoon butter, melted

Melt 2 tablespoons butter with the flour in a saucepan over low heat, stirring constantly. Remove from the heat. Stir in the sugar, salt, pepper, onion and sour cream. Fold in the green beans. Spoon into a 2-quart baking dish. Cover with the cheese. Mix the cornflake crumbs and 1 tablespoon butter in a bowl. Sprinkle over the cheese. Bake at 350 degrees for 30 minutes. SERVES 4

Mediterranean Green Beans

5 slices bacon
1 onion, chopped
1 garlic clove, chopped
2 (16-ounce) cans green beans, drained
1 (15-ounce) can chopped tomatoes
1 tablespoon dry mustard
Salt and pepper to taste

Fry the bacon with the onion and garlic in a skillet until the bacon is crisp. Remove the bacon from the skillet to paper towels to drain. Add the green beans, tomatoes, dry mustard, salt and pepper to the onion mixture in the skillet and stir to mix well. Simmer for 30 minutes. Crumble the bacon and sprinkle over the top. SERVES 8

Tomato Feta Green Beans

¹/₄ cup pine nuts
2 pounds fresh green beans, trimmed
2 garlic cloves, minced
2 teaspoons Italian seasoning
1 tablespoon Bertolli olive oil
4 plum tomatoes, chopped
2 tablespoons lemon juice
1 teaspoon salt
¹/₂ teaspoon pepper
1 (4-ounce) package crumbled feta cheese

Spread the pine nuts in a shallow baking pan. Bake at 350 degrees for 6 to 8 minutes or until toasted.

Boil the green beans in water to cover in a saucepan until tender-crisp; drain and blot with paper towels. Sauté the garlic and Italian seasoning in the hot olive oil in a skillet over medium heat for 1 minute. Add the green beans. Sauté for 5 minutes. Stir in the tomatoes. Cook until heated through. Stir in the lemon juice, salt and pepper. Sprinkle with the cheese and toasted pine nuts. Serve immediately. SERVES 6 TO 8

Stuffed Portobello Mushroom

CHEF TONY RAHILL

Chef Tony Rahill earned his culinary credentials at the Walt Disney World Culinary School and worked at Disney World Resorts for seven years before moving to Owensboro. One of Tony's many specialties is his Stuffed Portobello Mushroom (at left).

SWEET VERMOUTH DEMI-GLAZE

1 tablespoon chopped shallot or finely chopped red onion
1/4 cup sweet vermouth

1 cup beef stock
1 tablespoon cornstarch
1 tablespoon cold water
Salt and pepper to taste

PORTOBELLO MUSHROOM

1 large Portobello mushroom
1 tablespoon Bertolli olive oil
Salt and pepper to taste
3 ounces Crab Meat Stuffing (sidebar)

Herb butter to taste
1 (1/2-ounce) slice provolone cheese
1 1/2 teaspoons grated Parmesan cheese
Toasted round bread crouton

For the demi-glaze, sauté the shallot in a saucepan until translucent. Add the vermouth, stirring to deglaze the saucepan. Simmer for 1 minute. Add the stock. Cook until the mixture is reduced by 1/2. Mix the cornstarch and water in a small cup. Stir into the stock mixture. Cook until thickened and glossy, stirring constantly. Season with salt and pepper.

For the mushroom, remove the stem from the mushroom. Brush the mushroom with the olive oil. Season with salt and pepper. Place on a grill rack. Grill for 1 to 2 minutes or until tender. (Do not overcook or the mushroom will lose its shape.)

Place the mushroom on a small baking sheet. Place the crab meat stuffing in the center of the mushroom. Brush with herb butter. Bake at 350 degrees for 5 minutes. Remove from the oven. Top with the provolone cheese. Sprinkle with the Parmesan cheese. Bake for 3 minutes.

Place the crouton in the center of a large plate. Top with the hot mushroom. Cover with 1/4 cup of the demi-glaze. Garnish with chopped fresh parsley. SERVES 1

NOTE: The demi-glaze makes 1/2 to 3/4 cup.

Crab Meat Stuffing

Mix 6 ounces imitation crab meat, 5 ounces seasoned bread crumbs, 1 ounce chopped yellow onion, 1 ounce chopped red and green bell peppers, 1/4 teaspoon ganulated garlic, 1 1/2 teaspoons lemon juice, 1/4 teaspoon Mrs. Dash, 1 egg, 1/2 teaspoon Dijon mustard, salt and pepper to taste in a bowl.

MAKES ABOUT
12 OUNCES

Mushroom and Cheese Stuffed Peppers

4 cups sliced fresh mushrooms
2 tablespoons vegetable oil
3 eggs
4 ounces Parmesan cheese, grated
1 pound Swiss cheese, shredded
1/4 cup chopped fresh parsley

1/2 cup finely chopped celery
6 large green bell peppers
1/4 cup vegetable oil
1 cup water
1 (7-ounce) jar pimentos, drained
  and chopped

Sauté the mushrooms in 2 tablespoons oil in a skillet until tender; drain and pat dry. Beat the eggs in a bowl. Add the mushrooms, Parmesan cheese, Swiss cheese, parsley and celery and mix well to form a paste.

Cut the bell peppers into halves lengthwise and discard the seeds. Spoon the mushroom paste into each bell pepper half. Place 2 tablespoons oil and 1/2 cup water in each of two 9×13-inch baking dishes. Arrange 6 stuffed bell peppers in a single layer in each prepared dish. Top each with the pimentos. Bake, covered with foil, at 350 degrees for 45 minutes. SERVES 12

NOTE: The mushroom paste and bell peppers can be prepared separately the day before and stored in the refrigerator.

Blue Cheese Vidalia Onions

2 large Vidalia onions, sliced
6 ounces blue cheese, crumbled
2 tablespoons butter, softened

2 teaspoons Worcestershire sauce
1/2 teaspoon dill weed
Pepper to taste

Arrange the onions in a 9×13-inch baking pan. Combine the cheese, butter, Worcestershire sauce, dill weed and pepper in a bowl and mix well. Spread over the onions. Bake, uncovered, at 425 degrees for 20 minutes. Broil until the cheese mixture is brown. SERVES 8

Marinated Vidalia Onions

2 Vidalia onions
1 cup water
1/2 cup sugar

1/4 cup white vinegar
4 teaspoons Hellmann's mayonnaise
1 teaspoon celery seeds

Cut the onions into slices and separate into rings. Place the onion rings in a large bowl. Combine the water, sugar and vinegar in a bowl and stir until the sugar dissolves. Pour over the onion rings. Marinate, covered, in the refrigerator for at least 3 hours. Drain the onions, discarding the marinade. Stir in the mayonnaise and celery seeds. Serve on lettuce leaves. SERVES 4

Creamy Mashed Potatoes

8 to 10 potatoes, peeled and chopped
Salt to taste
1/2 cup (1 stick) butter, softened
1/4 cup milk
1 cup sour cream

8 ounces cream cheese, softened
1 teaspoon garlic salt
1 teaspoon salt
3 to 4 tablespoons butter
Paprika to taste

Cook the potatoes in salted water to cover in a saucepan until tender; drain. Add 1/2 cup butter and the milk and mash until smooth. Beat in the sour cream, cream cheese, garlic salt and 1 teaspoon salt until smooth. Spoon into a greased 9×13-inch baking dish. Chill, covered, in the refrigerator for 24 hours. Remove from the refrigerator and let stand at room temperature for 2 to 3 hours. Top with 3 to 4 tablespoons butter. Sprinkle with paprika. Bake at 350 degrees for 30 minutes. SERVES 8

Muenster Potatoes

6 potatoes
2 cups (8 ounces) shredded
   Muenster cheese
1/4 cup (1/2 stick) butter
1 cup sour cream

1/3 cup finely chopped onion
1 teaspoon salt
1/4 teaspoon pepper
Paprika to taste

Scrub the potatoes. Cook in 1 inch of boiling water in a 3-quart saucepan until tender; drain. Peel the potatoes and shred into a bowl.

   Combine the cheese and butter in a 2-quart saucepan. Cook over low heat until almost melted, stirring constantly. Remove from the heat. Stir in the sour cream, onion, salt and pepper. Fold into the potatoes. Spoon into a greased 8×8-inch baking dish. Sprinkle with paprika. Bake at 350 degrees for 30 minutes. SERVES 8

NOTE: You may substitute one 16-ounce package frozen hash brown potatoes, thawed and shredded, for the potatoes.

Hot Potato Salad

8 to 10 red potatoes
Salt and pepper to taste
1 small Vidalia onion, sliced
5 eggs, hard-cooked and sliced

1 1/3 cups Hellmann's mayonnaise
1/3 cup sugar
3 tablespoons spicy brown mustard
8 slices bacon, crisp-cooked

Scrub the potatoes and cut into slices. Cook the potatoes in water to cover in a saucepan until tender; drain. Layer the potatoes in a 9×13-inch baking dish. Season generously with salt and pepper. Layer the onion and hard-cooked egg slices over the potatoes. Blend the mayonnaise, sugar and mustard in a bowl. Spread over the layers. Bake at 350 degrees for 25 minutes. Crumble the bacon and sprinkle over the top. Bake for 10 to 15 minutes or until golden brown. SERVES 8 TO 10

Sweet Potato Casserole

SWEET POTATOES

3 cups mashed cooked sweet potatoes
$1/2$ cup packed light brown sugar
$1/2$ teaspoon salt
2 eggs, beaten
$1/2$ cup evaporated milk
1 teaspoon vanilla extract
2 tablespoons plus 2 teaspoons ($1/3$ stick) butter or
  margarine, melted

TOPPING

$1/4$ cup ($1/2$ stick) butter or margarine
1 cup packed brown sugar
$1/3$ cup flour
1 cup chopped walnuts or pecans
1 cup shredded coconut (optional)

For the sweet potatoes, combine the sweet potatoes, brown sugar, salt, eggs, evaporated milk, vanilla and butter in a bowl and mix well. Spoon into a baking dish.

For the topping, cut the butter into the brown sugar and flour in a bowl until crumbly. Stir in the walnuts and coconut.

Sprinkle the topping over the sweet potato mixture. Bake at 350 degrees for 30 minutes. SERVES 6

When choosing produce at the store, purchase produce that is not bruised, shriveled, moldy, or slimy. Buy vegetables that have little or no liquid in the packaging. Buy only what you need because most fruits and vegetables should be used within a few days. Refrigerate unwashed produce promptly and within two hours after peeling or cutting. Wash all fresh fruits and vegetables with cool water immediately before eating. Scrub firm produce with a clean produce brush.

Yellow Squash Casserole

5 or 6 small squash, sliced
1 onion, chopped
8 ounces cream cheese, softened
3 tablespoons sugar
Salt to taste
$1/2$ cup (1 stick) butter or margarine, melted
2 stacks butter crackers, crushed

Cook the squash and onion in water to cover in a saucepan until tender; drain. Add the cream cheese, sugar and salt and mix well. Spoon into a buttered $1\frac{1}{2}$-quart baking dish. Combine the butter and crackers in a bowl and toss to coat. Sprinkle over the squash mixture. Bake at 325 degrees for 45 minutes. SERVES 8

Squash Patties

1 egg, beaten
1 tablespoon sugar
$1/2$ teaspoon salt
Dash of pepper
2 tablespoons milk
2 tablespoons finely chopped onion
1 cup mashed cooked squash
$1/2$ cup self-rising flour
Vegetable oil for frying

Combine the egg, sugar, salt, pepper, milk, onion, squash and flour in a bowl and mix well. Heat oil in a skillet. Drop the squash mixture by tablespoonfuls into the hot oil, flattening each patty to $1/4$ to $1/2$ inch thick. Fry until golden brown on each side, turning once. Remove to paper towels to drain. Serve warm. SERVES 14

Tomato Pie

1 unbaked (9-inch)
    pie shell
3 or 4 tomatoes, peeled
    and chopped into
    bite-size pieces
1 cup Hellmann's
    mayonnaise

1 cup (4 ounces) shredded
    Cheddar cheese
$1^1/2$ teaspoons each
    chopped fresh oregano,
    basil and parsley
$^1/2$ teaspoon salt
$^1/2$ teaspoon pepper

Prick the pie shell with a fork. Bake at 350 degrees for 10 minutes. Remove from the oven and maintain the oven temperature. Layer the tomatoes in the pie shell. Mix the mayonnaise, cheese, oregano, basil, parsley, salt and pepper in a bowl. Spread over the tomatoes. Bake for 25 to 30 minutes or until heated through.
SERVES 6 TO 8

Tomatoes to Die For

4 firm tomatoes
12 slices bacon, cut into
    pieces
$^1/2$ cup chopped green bell
    pepper
$^1/2$ cup finely chopped
    onion

6 ounces Cheddar cheese,
    shredded
2 tablespoons cracker
    crumbs or dry bread
    crumbs
1 tablespoon butter

Remove the tops of the tomatoes. Scoop out the pulp and reserve. Drain the tomato shells upside down on a wire rack. Cook the bacon in a skillet until almost cooked through; drain. Add the bell pepper and onion. Sauté until the onion is translucent. Remove from the heat. Stir in the cheese and reserved tomato pulp. Spoon into the tomato shells. Place in a buttered 9×13-inch baking dish. Sprinkle with the cracker crumbs and dot with the butter. Bake at 400 degrees for 30 minutes. SERVES 4

Green River Fried Green Tomatoes

Cut green tomatoes into very thin slices. Place in a bowl of salted cold water. Chill in the refrigerator for 2 to 4 hours. Shake each slice as it is removed from the water, but do not drain. Dredge in cornmeal until well coated. Fry in hot bacon grease or vegetable oil in a skillet until golden brown. Sprinkle with pepper to taste. Serve immediately.

MAKES A VARIABLE
AMOUNT

Tomatoes Vinaigrette

3 tablespoons Bertolli olive oil
1 cup red wine vinegar
1/2 cup (scant) sugar
1 or 2 garlic cloves, minced
1 tablespoon thyme
Dash of parsley
1 tablespoon salt
Pepper to taste
10 tomatoes

Combine the olive oil, vinegar, sugar, garlic, thyme, parsley, salt and pepper in a bowl and mix well. Cut the unpeeled tomatoes into quarters and place in a shallow dish. Cover with the marinade. Marinate, covered, in the refrigerator for 1 hour before serving.
SERVES 8 TO 10

Winter Vegetables with Mustard Sauce

2 cups cubed new red potatoes (6 potatoes)
1 cup sliced carrots
2 cups water
2 (10-ounce) packages frozen brussels sprouts
1/3 cup butter, melted
4 teaspoons country-style Dijon mustard
4 teaspoons white vinegar
1/2 teaspoon salt
1/4 teaspoon pepper
Dash of hot pepper sauce

Combine the potatoes, carrots and water in a 3-quart saucepan. Bring to a boil and reduce the heat to medium. Cook, covered, for 8 minutes. Add the brussels sprouts. Cook for 10 to 12 minutes or until the vegetables are tender-crisp, stirring occasionally; drain.

Mix the butter, Dijon mustard, vinegar, salt, pepper and hot pepper sauce in a bowl. Pour over the vegetables and toss to coat. SERVES 6

Artichoke Rice

1 (7-ounce) package chicken-flavored Rice-A-Roni
2 (6-ounce) jars marinated artichoke hearts
4 to 6 green onions, chopped
1/2 bell pepper, chopped
1 (4-ounce) jar stuffed green olives, drained and sliced
3/4 teaspoon curry powder
Dash of salt
Dash of garlic powder
1/4 cup Hellmann's mayonnaise

Cook the Rice-A-Roni using the package directions. Cool in the refrigerator. Drain the artichokes, reserving the marinade. Chop the artichokes in a bowl. Add the reserved marinade, green onions, bell pepper, olives, curry powder, salt, garlic powder and mayonnaise and mix well. Stir in the chilled Rice-A-Roni. Spoon into a serving bowl. Chill, covered, for 8 to 12 hours before serving. SERVES 4 TO 6

The Love House Rice

1/3 cup finely minced onion
2 tablespoons butter
1 cup uncooked white rice
2 cups chicken stock
Salt and pepper to taste
1/2 bay leaf
1/2 teaspoon thyme
1/2 teaspoon parsley

Sauté the onion in the butter in a saucepan over low heat until soft and translucent. Add the rice. Sauté over medium heat for 3 to 4 minutes or until the rice grains turn milky white. Stir in the stock. Season lightly with salt and pepper. Add the bay leaf, thyme and parsley. Return to a simmer, stirring briefly. Simmer, tightly covered, over medium heat for 18 minutes; do not stir. Remove from the heat. Discard the bay leaf. Fluff the rice with a fork. SERVES 4

Tomatoes and Rice

1 small zucchini, thinly sliced
2 tablespoons butter
1 (14-ounce) can stewed tomatoes, drained
1 cup long grain rice
1 cup water
1 teaspoon chicken bouillon granules

Sauté the zucchini in the butter in a skillet until tender-crisp. Stir in the tomatoes, rice, water and bouillon granules. Simmer, tightly covered, for 25 minutes or until the liquid is absorbed. SERVES 6

NOTE: This is a great casual, weeknight side dish.

Gruyère Grits Soufflé

4 cups (1 quart) milk
1/2 cup (1 stick) butter or margarine
3/4 cup (3 ounces) shredded Gruyère cheese
1 cup uncooked grits
1 teaspoon salt
1/8 teaspoon black pepper
Dash of cayenne pepper or Tabasco sauce
1/3 cup margarine, melted
1/2 cup (2 ounces) grated Parmesan cheese

Bring the milk to a boil in a large saucepan. Add the butter and Gruyère cheese. Cook until melted, stirring constantly. Add the grits, salt, black pepper and cayenne pepper. Cook until thickened, stirring constantly. Remove from the heat. Beat for 5 minutes. Pour into a greased 2-quart soufflé dish. Pour the margarine over the top. Sprinkle with the Parmesan cheese. Bake at 375 degrees for 30 minutes or until firm. SERVES 6

Lemon Risotto

5 cups chicken stock
Sprig of fresh mint
Sprig of fresh rosemary
Sprig of fresh sage
Grated zest of 1 lemon
2 tablespoons unsalted
  butter
1 tablespoon Bertolli
  extra-virgin olive oil
2 shallots, minced
$1/8$ teaspoon salt

$1^1/2$ cups uncooked
  Italian arborio rice
2 tablespoons unsalted
  butter
3 tablespoons freshly
  squeezed lemon juice
$1/2$ cup (2 ounces)
  freshly grated Italian
  Parmigiano-Reggiano
  cheese

Bring the stock to a simmer in a large saucepan. Remove the leaves from the sprigs of the fresh herbs, discarding the stems. Chop the herb leaves and lemon zest finely.

Combine 2 tablespoons butter, the olive oil, shallots and salt in a large heavy saucepan. Sauté over medium heat for 3 minutes or until the shallots are soft and translucent. Add the rice. Cook for 1 to 2 minutes or until the rice is well coated, glistening and almost translucent, stirring constantly. Add a ladleful of the simmering stock. Cook for 1 to 2 minutes or until the rice has absorbed most of the stock, stirring constantly. Add another ladleful of the simmering stock. Cook for 1 to 2 minutes or until the rice has absorbed most of the stock, stirring constantly. Adjust the heat to maintain a gentle simmer. Repeat until all of the remaining stock has been absorbed and the rice is almost tender but firm to the bite, stirring frequently. (The total cooking time for the remaining stock to be absorbed is about 17 minutes. The risotto should be creamy.)

Remove the saucepan from the heat. Stir in 2 tablespoons butter, the herb and lemon zest mixture, lemon juice and cheese. Let stand, covered, for 2 minutes. Spoon immediately into shallow serving bowls and garnish with additional Parmigiano-Reggiano cheese. SERVES 4 TO 6

Risotto Cakes

Risotto is an Italian rice dish made with strains of short grain rice, broth, and other ingredients that give it flavor. But with its incomparable consistency of firm rice grains bound in a velvety sauce, risotto is hardly ordinary. Cooking risotto is a slow process that produces a creamy and smooth sauce. Leftover risotto will lose much of its original texture and appeal. However, leftover risotto may be used to prepare delicious risotto cakes. Simply take $1/2$ cup of the risotto and shape into a disc. Make an indentation in the center with your thumb. Pack with 1 tablespoon diced mozzarella cheese. Carefully cover the cheese with the risotto, making sure that the cheese is not exposed. Dip the cake into a beaten egg in a shallow dish, then coat with bread crumbs. Fry in Bertolli olive oil in a skillet until brown.

Romaine Soufflé

A successful soufflé, golden brown and puffy, is a triumph of the cook's art, rising high above the rim of its dish in apparent disregard of gravity. A soufflé is made by mixing a highly flavored sauce with stiffly whipped egg whites, which expand in a hot oven to give the mixture dramatic height. Three points are crucial: a soufflé base of the right consistency, egg whites that are stiffly beaten, and careful folding of the two together so as to retain maximum volume and lightness.

1 head romaine, trimmed and coarsely chopped
1 tablespoon butter
1/4 cup chopped shallots
3 tablespoons butter
3 tablespoons flour
1 cup milk, heated
1 cup (4 ounces) shredded Gruyère cheese
4 egg yolks
1 teaspoon salt
1 teaspoon Worcestershire sauce
8 drops of hot pepper sauce
5 egg whites, stiffly beaten
Grated Parmesan cheese to taste

Cook the romaine in a heavy nonstick saucepan until wilted; drain and chop finely. Melt 1 tablespoon butter in a skillet. Add the shallots. Sauté until soft. Add the romaine. Cook until dry, stirring constantly. Spoon into a sieve and press out the excess moisture.

Melt 3 tablespoons butter in a saucepan. Stir in the flour. Cook for several minutes, stirring constantly. Remove from the heat. Whisk in the milk. Return to the heat. Cook until thickened, stirring constantly. Add the Gruyère cheese. Cook until melted. Remove from the heat. Whisk in the egg yolks 1 at a time. Return to the heat. Cook for 1 minute. Add the romaine mixture, salt, Worcestershire sauce and hot pepper sauce. Stir in 1/3 of the stiffly beaten egg whites. Fold in the remaining stiffly beaten egg whites.

Butter a 1 1/2-quart soufflé dish. Coat with Parmesan cheese. Spoon the romaine mixture into the prepared dish. Sprinkle with Parmesan cheese. Place in a 400-degree oven. Reduce the oven temperature to 375 degrees. Bake for 35 to 40 minutes or until light brown. Serve immediately. SERVES 6 TO 8

Entrées

Marinara

14 ounces fresh
  mushrooms, cut into
  quarters
13 ounces onions, minced
4 ounces green bell
  pepper, minced
4 cups red wine
1 (10-ounce) can
  marinara

1 (28-ounce) can diced
  tomatoes
2 teaspoons basil
2 teaspoons oregano
2 teaspoons thyme
2 teaspoons salt
2 teaspoons pepper
2 teaspoons sugar

Sauté the mushrooms, onions and bell pepper in a skillet over high heat until the bottom of the pan begins to brown. Stir in the wine. Cook until the liquid is reduced by 1/2, stirring constantly. Add the remaining ingredients and mix well. Simmer for 1 hour, stirring occasionally. Spoon the sauce over hot cooked pasta. SERVES 4 TO 6

Pasta Shells Florentine

1 (10-ounce) package
  frozen chopped spinach,
  thawed and well drained
1 cup (4 ounces)
  shredded mozzarella
  cheese
1 cup low-fat cottage
  cheese

1 tablespoon grated
  Parmesan cheese
1 egg white, lightly beaten
1/4 teaspoon nutmeg
16 jumbo pasta shells,
  cooked and drained
1 jar Ragú spaghetti
  sauce

Combine the spinach, cheeses, egg white and nutmeg in a bowl and mix well. Fill each pasta shell with 1 heaping tablespoon of the spinach mixture.

Arrange the shells stuffing side up in a single layer in an 8×12-inch baking dish. Spoon the spaghetti sauce over the top. Bake, covered with foil, at 375 degrees for 30 to 40 minutes or until bubbly. SERVES 4

CHEF BRIAN JONES,
THE CAMPBELL CLUB

Marinara (at left) comes from the kitchen of Chef Brian Jones of The Campbell Club, a private dinner club in downtown Owensboro. The name honors Mary Campbell, the paternal grandmother of the founder, Marshall S. Burlew. The Campbell Club suggests a somewhat casual atmosphere at lunch and then turns more formal in the evening with chef specials and unique desserts.

Grilled Beef Tenderloin with Mushrooms

Steak Butter

Mix ½ cup softened butter, 1½ tablespoons Dijon mustard, 1 tablespoon chopped fresh chives and fresh cracked pepper to taste in a bowl. Top steaks with a dollop of the butter just before serving. You may spoon the butter into decorative molds for pretty accents.

MAKES ½ CUP

1 pound fresh mushrooms, sliced
1 cup chopped green onions
¼ cup (½ stick) butter or margarine
¼ cup chopped fresh parsley
1 (6- to 7-pound) beef tenderloin
½ teaspoon Lawry's seasoned salt
¼ teaspoon Lawry's lemon pepper
4 ounces blue cheese, crumbled
1 (8-ounce) bottle Wish-Bone red wine vinaigrette
Crushed peppercorns to taste

Sauté the mushrooms and green onions in the butter in a large skillet until tender; drain. Stir in the parsley. Set aside.

Trim the excess fat from the tenderloin. Cut the tenderloin lengthwise to within ¼ inch of the bottom, leaving 1 long side connected. Sprinkle with the seasoned salt and lemon pepper. Spread the mushroom mixture on 1 cut side of the tenderloin and sprinkle with the cheese. Press the sides together and secure with kitchen twine at 2-inch intervals.

Arrange the tenderloin in a large shallow dish and pour the vinaigrette over the top. Marinate, covered, in the refrigerator for 8 hours, basting with the vinaigrette occasionally. Remove the tenderloin from the dish and discard the marinade. Press peppercorns over the surface of the tenderloin. Grill, covered or tented, over medium-hot coals for 35 minutes or until a meat thermometer registers 145 degrees for rare or 160 degrees for medium. Remove the tenderloin to a serving platter and discard the twine. Let rest for 10 to 15 minutes before serving.
SERVES 8 TO 10

NOTE: Tenderloin may be baked at 350 degrees for 40 minutes or until a meat thermometer registers 145 to 160 degrees.

Grilled Kentucky Bourbon Beef Tenderloin

1 (8-pound) beef tenderloin
2 garlic cloves, chopped
1 tablespoon freshly ground pepper
2 teaspoons Lawry's seasoned salt
1 cup vegetable oil

1 cup bourbon
3/4 cup Worcestershire sauce
2 tablespoons dry mustard
2 tablespoons chopped fresh parsley

Rub the tenderloin with the garlic, pepper and seasoned salt. Place the tenderloin in a large shallow dish. Combine the oil, bourbon, Worcestershire sauce, dry mustard and parsley in a bowl and mix well. Pour the oil mixture over the tenderloin, turning to coat.

Marinate, covered, in the refrigerator for 8 hours or longer, turning occasionally. Arrange the tenderloin on a grill rack. Sear over high heat; reduce the heat to low. Grill for 20 to 25 minutes for medium-rare or to the desired degree of doneness. Let rest for 10 to 15 minutes before slicing. SERVES 15

NOTE: Letting meat "rest" allows the juices to retract back into the meat, creating a juicier and more tender finished product.

Stuffed Steak Tortillas

1 (1½-pound) flank steak
1 (8-ounce) bottle Wish-Bone vinaigrette
1 teaspoon cumin

8 ounces pepper cheese, cut lengthwise
   into 8 slices
8 (8-inch) flour tortillas

Cut a slit horizontally in the steak to form a pocket, cutting to within ½ inch of but not through the opposite edge. Mix the vinaigrette and cumin in a shallow dish. Add the steak to the vinaigrette mixture and turn to coat.

Marinate, covered, in the refrigerator for 3 hours, turning occasionally. Drain, discarding the marinade. Place the cheese slices in the steak pocket and secure with wooden picks. Grill, with the lid closed, over medium-high heat for 7 to 10 minutes on each side. Let stand for 5 minutes.

Discard the wooden picks and cut the steak diagonally into thin strips. Grill the tortillas for 1 to 2 minutes on each side. Arrange the steak strips on the tortillas and roll to enclose. SERVES 4

Green Peppercorn Mayonnaise

Rehydrate 2 tablespoons whole green peppercorns in hot water in a small bowl for 5 minutes; drain. Pat dry with a paper towel. Crush 1 tablespoon dry green peppercorns until the consistency of coarse pepper. Mix the rehydrated peppercorns, crushed peppercorns and 1 cup Hellmann's mayonnaise in a bowl. Chill, covered, until serving time. Serve with sliced tenderloin or spread on a roast beef sandwich.

MAKES 1 CUP

Dinner in a Pumpkin

1 small to medium pumpkin
1¹/₂ to 2 pounds ground beef
1 small onion, chopped
³/₄ cup chopped celery
¹/₃ cup chopped green bell pepper
1 (10-ounce) can cream of chicken soup
1 (4-ounce) can sliced mushrooms, drained

2 tablespoons brown sugar
2 teaspoons soy sauce
1 teaspoon salt
¹/₄ teaspoon pepper
1¹/₂ cups cooked brown rice
1 (8-ounce) can sliced water chestnuts, drained

Cut the top from the pumpkin and reserve. Remove the seeds and membranes from the pumpkin. Brown the ground beef in a skillet, stirring until crumbly; drain. Stir in the onion, celery and bell pepper.

Cook until the onion is tender, stirring frequently. Add the soup, mushrooms, brown sugar, soy sauce, salt and pepper and mix well. Simmer for 10 minutes, stirring occasionally. Stir in the rice and water chestnuts.

Spoon the ground beef mixture into the pumpkin and replace the top. Arrange the pumpkin on a baking sheet. Bake at 350 degrees for 1 to 1¹/₂ hours or until the inside pumpkin pulp is tender. Place the pumpkin on a serving platter and remove the top. Serve immediately. SERVES 6

Saucy Stuffed Shells with Four Cheeses

1 pound ground beef
1 pound Italian sausage
1 teaspoon garlic salt
3 cups water
3 (6-ounce) cans tomato paste
1 teaspoon salt
1/2 teaspoon pepper
1/2 teaspoon Italian seasoning
1/2 teaspoon basil
16 ounces ricotta cheese
2 eggs, lightly beaten
3 cups (12 ounces) shredded mozzarella cheese
1 cup (4 ounces) grated Parmesan cheese
Jumbo pasta shells, cooked and drained
8 slices provolone cheese

Brown the ground beef and sausage with the garlic salt in a skillet over medium heat, stirring until the ground beef and sausage are crumbly; drain. Stir in the water, tomato paste, salt, pepper, Italian seasoning and basil. Simmer for 1 hour, stirring occasionally.

Combine the ricotta cheese and eggs in a bowl and mix well. Stir in the mozzarella cheese and Parmesan cheese. Fill the pasta shells generously with the cheese mixture; the shells will be overflowing with the stuffing. Arrange the shells stuffing side up in a single layer in a 9×13-inch baking dish sprayed lightly with nonstick cooking spray. Arrange the provolone cheese slices over the top and spread with the ground beef mixture.

Bake, covered, at 350 degrees for 45 minutes; remove the cover. Bake for 15 minutes longer. Let stand at room temperature for 10 to 15 minutes before serving. Serve with additional Parmesan cheese, if desired. SERVES 12

Grilled Boneless Lamb

1 small onion, grated
1/2 cup water
1/3 cup ketchup
1/4 cup lemon juice
2 tablespoons vinegar
1 garlic clove, minced
1 tablespoon Worcestershire sauce

1 tablespoon vegetable oil
1 teaspoon dry mustard
1/2 teaspoon salt
1/4 teaspoon paprika
1/8 teaspoon Tabasco sauce
1 leg of lamb, boned and rolled

Bring the onion, water, ketchup, lemon juice, vinegar, garlic, Worcestershire sauce, oil, dry mustard, salt, paprika and Tabasco sauce to a boil in a saucepan. Boil for several minutes. Place the lamb in a large shallow dish. Pour the onion mixture over the lamb.

   Marinate, covered, in the refrigerator for 2 to 3 days, turning occasionally. Drain, reserving the marinade. Grill the lamb over hot coals for 2 hours or until a meat thermometer registers 145 degrees for medium-rare or 160 degrees for medium, turning and basting with the reserved marinade frequently. Serve with mint jelly. You may bake in the oven, if desired. SERVES 8 TO 12

Bourbon-Marinated Pork Tenderloin

2 to 3 pounds pork tenderloin
1/4 cup soy sauce
1/4 cup bourbon
1/4 cup packed brown sugar
1/4 cup vegetable oil

1/4 cup Dijon mustard
3 garlic cloves, minced
1 teaspoon Worcestershire sauce
1/2 teaspoon salt

Place the pork in a 1-gallon resealable plastic bag. Mix the soy sauce, bourbon, brown sugar, oil, Dijon mustard, garlic, Worcestershire sauce and salt in a bowl. Pour the soy sauce mixture over the pork and seal tightly. Turn to coat.

   Marinate in the refrigerator for 2 to 3 days, turning the bag occasionally; drain, discarding the marinade. Grill the pork over medium-hot coals for 20 to 25 minutes or until the center is no longer pink and a meat thermometer registers 160 degrees. Let stand for 10 minutes before slicing. SERVES 6 TO 8

Pork Tenderloin by Request

4 pounds boneless pork tenderloin
1/4 cup flour
1 tablespoon vegetable oil
2 tablespoons butter
1 3/4 cups currant jelly
2 to 3 teaspoons rosemary
1 1/2 teaspoons salt
1/2 teaspoon freshly ground pepper
2 cups heavy cream
2 tablespoons flour
Saffron Rice (sidebar)

Coat the pork lightly with 1/4 cup flour. Brown the pork on all sides in the oil in a roasting pan over medium-high heat. Spread the butter and jelly over the surface of the pork. Sprinkle with the rosemary, salt and pepper.

Bake, covered with foil, at 350 degrees for 45 to 60 minutes or until a meat thermometer registers 145 degrees. Remove the pork to a platter and cover to keep warm, reserving the pan drippings.

Mix the cream and 2 tablespoons flour in a small bowl. Add the cream mixture to the reserved pan drippings and mix well. Return the pork to the roasting pan. Bake, covered, for 15 minutes longer or until a meat thermometer registers 160 degrees. Remove the pork to a serving platter. Let stand for 15 minutes before serving. Serve with the sauce and Saffron Rice. SERVES 8

Saffron Rice

Bring a large saucepan of water, 2 teaspoons salt and 1 teaspoon saffron to a boil. Stir in 1 cup long grain rice gradually. Cook for 15 minutes or until the rice is tender; drain. Add 8 tablespoons butter and stir until melted.

SERVES 8

Smoked Baby Back Ribs

6 slabs baby back ribs, cut into halves
1 1/4 cups honey

1 (2-ounce) jar Lawry's lemon pepper
5 cups barbecue sauce

Coat the ribs on both sides with the honey and sprinkle with lemon pepper. Arrange the ribs in a roasting pan. Bake at 350 degrees for 30 minutes.

As the ribs are baking, start the coals using the water smoker directions. Use 10 pounds of charcoal and fill the water pan to the top. When the coals are ready, the temperature gauge will register warm. Add a handful of soaked mesquite wood chips. Place the ribs meat side up on the racks. Smoke, covered, for 2 hours. Do not peek.

Remove the ribs from the smoker, noting which slabs were on the bottom. Fill the water pan to the top with hot water. Baste the ribs with approximately 1 1/4 cups of the barbecue sauce. Return the ribs to the racks in the reverse order, so the slabs that were nearest the water pan are now on top. Smoke for 2 hours longer, checking the water pan periodically and refilling as needed. The ribs will be ready sometime between the fourth and fifth hour. The finished ribs should be dry and nearly fat free, but still moist and juicy.

Remove the ribs from the smoker and baste with 1 1/4 cups of the remaining barbecue sauce. Place the ribs in a roasting pan and cover with foil. The ribs will hold for 3 to 4 hours or even up to overnight. Reheat in a 250-degree oven before serving if needed. Warm the remaining barbecue sauce in a saucepan and serve with the ribs for dipping. SERVES 8 TO 10

Easy and Elegant Ham

2 (15-ounce) cans juice-pack sliced
  pineapple
1 (6-pound) cooked boneless ham

1 (6-ounce) jar maraschino cherries,
  drained
1 (12-ounce) jar orange marmalade

Drain the pineapple, reserving the juice. Place 1/2 of the pineapple in a 5-quart slow cooker. Arrange the ham over the pineapple and sprinkle with the cherries. Top with the remaining pineapple, reserved pineapple juice and marmalade.

Cook, covered, on Low for 6 to 7 hours or until heated through. Remove the ham to a heated serving platter. Arrange the pineapple and cherries around the ham. Let stand for 10 to 15 minutes before slicing. SERVES 8 TO 10

Pasta Peyton

16 ounces farfalle
1 pound prosciutto, chopped
1 pound fresh asparagus, trimmed, blanched and
* sliced*
3 garlic cloves, chopped
1/2 teaspoon red pepper flakes
6 to 7 tablespoons Bertolli olive oil
1 cup (4 ounces) grated Parmesan cheese

Cook the pasta using the package directions until al
dente; drain. Sauté the prosciutto, asparagus, garlic and
red pepper flakes in 2 tablespoons of the olive oil in a
skillet for 2 to 3 minutes.

Toss the pasta with the remaining olive oil. Add the
pasta to the prosciutto mixture and mix well. Cook just
until heated through, stirring frequently. Spoon into a
pasta bowl and sprinkle with the cheese. SERVES 4

Produced only in the
Parma province of Italy,
prosciutto is ham cured
solely with salt and aged
ten months to two years.
Each step of the process
is dictated by law and
overseen by the Parma
Ham Consortium.
Fragrant and sweet with
delicate, complex
aromas, prosciutto
should be soft pink to
deep rose with a fine
marbling of fat. Sliced
prosciutto should be
consumed as soon as
possible and, if possible,
removed from the
refrigerator one hour
before serving.

Not Your Mom's Meat Loaf

1/2 cup each chopped onion, celery and
  carrots
2 garlic cloves, minced
1 tablespoon vegetable oil
1 1/2 pounds ground beef
8 ounces sweet Italian sausage, casings
  removed
1/2 cup dry bread crumbs

1/2 cup milk
1/4 cup ketchup
2 eggs, lightly beaten
1 tablespoon Dijon mustard
1 teaspoon chopped fresh rosemary
1/2 teaspoon salt
1/2 teaspoon pepper
3 tablespoons ketchup

Sauté the onion, celery, carrots and garlic in the oil in a skillet over medium heat for 8 minutes. Let stand until cool. Mix the onion mixture, ground beef, sausage, bread crumbs, milk, 1/4 cup ketchup, eggs, Dijon mustard, rosemary, salt and pepper in a bowl.

Shape into a loaf in a 4×8-inch loaf pan and spread the top with 3 tablespoons ketchup. Bake at 350 degrees for 1 1/4 hours. Let stand for 15 minutes before serving. SERVES 6

Red Beans and Rice with Sausage

1 pound dried red beans, sorted and
  rinsed, or 4 (16-ounce) cans red beans
Salt to taste
16 cups water
1 pound smoked sausage, chopped
1 onion, chopped
2 bay leaves

3 large garlic cloves, chopped, or
  1 1/2 teaspoons minced garlic
1 1/2 teaspoons thyme
1 teaspoon cayenne pepper
1 teaspoon black pepper
3/4 tablespoon Lawry's seasoned salt
Hot cooked rice

Soak the beans in 8 cups lightly salted water in a bowl for 8 to 10 hours, or bring the beans and 8 cups lightly salted water to a boil in a large saucepan. Boil for 5 minutes. Remove from the heat. Let stand, covered, for 1 hour; drain. Combine the beans with the remaining 8 cups water. Bring to a low boil. Boil for 1 hour, stirring frequently. If you prefer to use canned beans, combine the undrained beans in a saucepan, adding approximately 1 cup of water if needed, and bring to a low boil. Add the sausage, onion and bay leaves to the dried beans or canned beans and mix well. Cook for 1 hour, stirring frequently and adding water 1/4 cup at a time if the mixture becomes too thick. Stir in the next 5 ingredients. Cook for 30 minutes longer or until thickened, stirring constantly. Discard the bay leaves and spoon over hot cooked rice in bowls. SERVES 4

Creamy Ham and Chicken Lasagna

2 boneless skinless chicken breasts
2 cups chopped cooked ham
9 lasagna noodles
1 tablespoon butter or margarine
1 (14-ounce) can asparagus spears, drained and
  cut into bite-size pieces
8 ounces fresh mushrooms, sliced
1/3 cup butter or margarine
1/3 cup flour
3 cups milk
1 1/2 cups (6 ounces) grated Parmesan cheese
1/2 cup heavy cream
3/4 teaspoon dried basil, or 2 teaspoons chopped fresh basil
1/2 teaspoon salt
1/4 teaspoon pepper

Combine the chicken with enough water to cover in a saucepan. Bring to a boil; reduce the heat to medium. Cook, covered, for 45 minutes or until tender; drain. Let stand until cool. Chop the chicken into bite-size pieces and combine with the ham in a bowl.

Cook the noodles using the package directions; drain. Line a baking sheet with waxed paper and spray with nonstick cooking spray. Arrange the noodles in a single layer on the waxed paper, adding additional sheets of waxed paper sprayed with nonstick cooking spray as needed to separate the noodles.

Heat 1 tablespoon butter in a skillet. Stir in the asparagus and mushrooms and cook until tender, stirring frequently; drain. Add the asparagus mixture to the chicken mixture and mix gently. Melt 1/3 cup butter in a skillet and stir in the flour. Cook for 1 minute, stirring constantly. Add the milk gradually, stirring constantly. Cook for 3 minutes or until bubbly, stirring constantly. Add the cheese, cream, basil, salt and pepper and mix well.

Cook until the cheese melts and the mixture thickens, stirring constantly. Add the chicken mixture to the cheese sauce and mix well. Layer the chicken mixture and noodles 1/3 at a time in a 2-quart baking dish sprayed with nonstick cooking spray. Bake, covered, at 350 degrees for 30 minutes. Let stand for 10 minutes before serving. Garnish with paprika and fresh parsley. SERVES 8

Chicken Romano

36 butter crackers, crushed
¹/₂ cup (2 ounces) grated Romano cheese
1 teaspoon garlic powder
2 (3-pound) chickens, cut up, or 12 to 14 chicken pieces
Salt to taste
¹/₂ cup (1 stick) margarine, melted

Mix the cracker crumbs, cheese and garlic powder in a shallow dish. Sprinkle the chicken with salt and dip into the margarine. Coat with the crumb mixture. Arrange the chicken in a single layer in a 9×15-inch baking pan. Bake at 350 degrees for 1 hour. SERVES 6 TO 8

Garlic Chicken Wings

2 pounds chicken wings
1 teaspoon salt
1 tablespoon Bertolli olive oil
8 large garlic cloves, minced
³/₄ cup banana pepper rings
1 tablespoon minced fresh parsley
¹/₄ cup red wine vinegar

Sprinkle the chicken with salt. Sauté the chicken in the olive oil in a skillet for 20 minutes; turn. Sauté for 15 to 20 minutes longer or until cooked through. Add the garlic, banana pepper rings and parsley.

Cook, covered, for 2 minutes; drizzle with the vinegar. Cook for 2 minutes longer, stirring occasionally. You may substitute 1 pound boneless skinless chicken breasts cut into bite-size pieces for the chicken wings. Sauté for 10 to 15 minutes or until cooked through. SERVES 4 TO 6

NOTE: This recipe is easily doubled. For an easy cleanup, omit the olive oil and place all the remaining ingredients in a slow cooker. Cook on Low for 6 to 8 hours or until the chicken is tender.

Stuffed Chicken Breasts with Herbed Pasta

TOMATO SAUCE

3 garlic cloves, minced
3 tablespoons Bertolli extra-virgin olive oil
1 (28-ounce) can Italian stewed tomatoes, finely chopped

3 tablespoons vermouth (optional)
2 tablespoons minced fresh parsley
1 chicken bouillon cube
1/2 teaspoon basil

CHICKEN

4 boneless skinless chicken breasts
Salt and pepper to taste
Garlic powder to taste
4 tablespoons Quick Pesto (sidebar)

Flour
2 tablespoons Bertolli extra-virgin olive oil
1 tablespoon unsalted butter

HERBED PASTA

9 ounces fettuccini, cooked and drained
2 tablespoons unsalted butter

2 tablespoons chopped fresh parsley
Garlic powder to taste

For the sauce, sauté the garlic in the olive oil in a saucepan. Stir in the undrained tomatoes, vermouth, parsley, bouillon cube and basil. Simmer for 20 minutes, stirring occasionally.

For the chicken, pound the chicken 1/4 inch thick between sheets of waxed paper. Season with salt, pepper and garlic powder. Place 1 tablespoon of the Quick Pesto on each and roll to enclose. Secure with wooden picks.

Coat the stuffed chicken breasts with flour. Brown in a mixture of the olive oil and butter in a skillet for 8 minutes and cover. Cook for 6 minutes longer or until the chicken is cooked through.

For the pasta, toss the hot pasta with the butter, parsley and garlic powder in a bowl. Divide the pasta evenly among 4 dinner plates. Top each serving with 1 stuffed chicken breast and drizzle with the sauce. SERVES 4

Quick Pesto

Mix 1/4 cup Bertolli extra-virgin olive oil, 1/4 cup softened unsalted butter, 1/4 cup freshly grated Parmesan cheese, 1/4 cup finely ground walnuts, 1/2 teaspoon marjoram, 1/2 cup minced fresh parsley, 1/2 teaspoon thyme and 1 minced garlic clove in a bowl. Store, covered, in the refrigerator.

MAKES 1 CUP

Chicken Parmesan with Spaghetti

Grandaddy Murphy's Dip

Combine the juice of 12 lemons, 1½ gallons vinegar, 3 pints Worcestershire sauce, 8 ounces black pepper, one 1⅞-ounce can red pepper, 2 pints salt, 1 quart water and 3 packages pickling spices tied in cheesecloth in a large stockpot. Bring to a boil. Boil for 30 minutes. Add 5 pounds butter. Heat until the butter melts, stirring occasionally. Discard the cheesecloth and store in gallon jars in the refrigerator. Use as a baste for chicken and mutton. Great recipe to prepare at the beginning of the summer and use all season.

MAKES 3 GALLONS

SAUCE

2 garlic cloves, minced
¼ cup Bertolli extra-virgin olive oil
½ teaspoon basil
¼ teaspoon oregano
¼ teaspoon sugar
Salt and pepper to taste
1 (28-ounce) can crushed tomatoes

CHICKEN AND ASSEMBLY

1 egg
Salt to taste
½ to 1 cup dry bread crumbs
¼ teaspoon salt
⅛ teaspoon pepper
2 large boneless skinless chicken breasts, cut into 4 cutlets
¼ cup Bertolli olive oil
¾ cup (3 ounces) shredded mozzarella cheese
¼ cup (1 ounce) grated Parmesan cheese
8 ounces spaghetti, cooked and drained

For the sauce, sauté the garlic in the olive oil in a saucepan until the garlic starts to sizzle. Stir in the seasonings and undrained tomatoes. Bring to a simmer, stirring frequently. Simmer for 10 minutes or until thickened, stirring frequently. Remove from the heat and cover to keep warm.

For the chicken, whisk the egg and salt to taste in a shallow dish until blended. Mix the bread crumbs, ¼ teaspoon salt and pepper in a shallow dish.

Dip the chicken into the egg and coat with the bread crumb mixture. Sauté the chicken in the olive oil in a 12-inch skillet over medium-high heat until golden brown on both sides, turning once. Remove the chicken to a rack positioned over a baking sheet. Top each with ¼ of the mozzarella cheese and ¼ of the Parmesan cheese.

Broil 4 to 5 inches from the heat source for 3 minutes or until the cheese melts and is spotty brown. Arrange 1 chicken cutlet and ¼ of the spaghetti on each of 4 dinner plates. Drizzle the sauce over the chicken and spaghetti. Sprinkle with additional Parmesan cheese. Serve immediately. SERVES 4

Country-Style Chicken Kiev

CHICKEN

2/3 cup butter

1/2 cup dry bread crumbs

1/4 cup (1 ounce) grated Parmesan
  cheese

4 teaspoons oregano

4 teaspoons basil

1/2 teaspoon garlic powder

1/4 teaspoon salt

6 chicken breasts

SAUCE

1/4 cup apple juice

1/4 cup chopped fresh parsley

1/4 cup chopped green onions

1/4 cup (1/2 stick) butter, melted

For the chicken, melt the butter in a shallow dish. Mix the bread crumbs, cheese, oregano, basil, garlic powder and salt in a shallow dish. Dip the chicken into the butter and coat with the bread crumb mixture. Arrange the chicken in a single layer in a large baking dish. Bake at 375 degrees for 45 to 50 minutes or until cooked through.

For the sauce, combine the apple juice, parsley, green onions and butter in a bowl and mix well. Drizzle the juice mixture over the hot chicken. Bake for 5 minutes longer.
SERVES 6

Chicken Piquant

1 pound fresh mushrooms

4 chicken breasts

2 tablespoons cornstarch

1/4 cup water

3/4 cup red wine

1/4 cup soy sauce

2 tablespoons Bertolli olive oil

2 tablespoons brown sugar

1 teaspoon minced garlic

1/4 teaspoon oregano

Line the bottom of a 9×13-inch baking dish with the mushrooms. Layer the chicken breasts over the mushrooms. Dissolve the cornstarch in the water. Mix the cornstarch mixture, wine, soy sauce, olive oil, brown sugar, garlic and oregano in a bowl and pour over the prepared layers. Bake at 350 degrees for 40 minutes or until the chicken is cooked through. SERVES 4

Golden Chicken Rolls

6 whole boneless skinless chicken breast
   fillets, split
12 thin slices cooked ham
12 thin slices Swiss cheese
1/2 cup (1 stick) butter or margarine,
   melted
1/4 cup (1 ounce) grated Parmesan
   cheese

2¹/₃ cups seasoned bread crumbs
1 cup undiluted cream of chicken soup
1 (4-ounce) can sliced mushrooms,
   drained
1/2 cup milk
2 tablespoons chives
1 cup sour cream

Open each chicken fillet and flatten between sheets of waxed paper. Layer each with 2 slices of the ham and 2 slices of the Swiss cheese. Roll to enclose the filling and secure with wooden picks. Dip the chicken rolls into the butter and coat with a mixture of the Parmesan cheese and bread crumbs. Arrange the chicken rolls in a 9×13-inch baking dish. Chill, covered, for 45 minutes. Bake at 400 degrees for 45 minutes.

    Combine the soup, mushrooms, milk and chives in a saucepan and mix well. Cook over medium heat until thickened, stirring frequently. Mix in the sour cream just before serving and drizzle over the chicken on dinner plates. SERVES 6

Summer Italian Chicken Pasta

8 ounces vermicelli
1¹/₂ cups Wish-Bone Italian dressing
3 cups chopped cooked chicken
1 (10-ounce) package frozen snow peas,
   thawed
15 fresh mushrooms, sliced

3/4 cup pine nuts
1/3 cup chopped fresh basil
1/4 cup chopped fresh parsley
1/4 teaspoon pepper
12 cherry tomatoes, cut into halves
8 ounces feta cheese, crumbled

Cook the pasta using the package directions; drain. Rinse with cold water and drain. Combine the pasta with 1/2 cup of the dressing in a bowl and toss to coat. Chill, covered, for 3 hours.

    Combine the remaining 1 cup dressing, chicken, snow peas, mushrooms, pine nuts, basil, parsley and pepper in a bowl and mix gently. Chill, covered, for 3 hours. To serve, toss the pasta mixture, chicken mixture and cherry tomatoes in a pasta bowl and sprinkle with the cheese. Serve chilled. SERVES 6

Company Chicken

1 (6-ounce) package wild rice
1 (10-ounce) package frozen chopped
   broccoli, thawed and drained
4 cups chopped cooked chicken
8 ounces fresh mushrooms, sliced
2 cups (8 ounces) shredded Cheddar
   cheese

1 (10-ounce) can cream of celery soup
1 cup Hellmann's mayonnaise
1 teaspoon curry powder
1/4 cup (1 ounce) grated Parmesan
   cheese

Prepare the rice using the package directions. Layer the rice, broccoli, chicken, mushrooms and Cheddar cheese in the order listed in a greased 9×13-inch baking dish. Combine the soup, mayonnaise and curry powder in a bowl and mix well. Spread the mayonnaise mixture over the prepared layers and sprinkle with the Parmesan cheese.

   Bake at 350 degrees for 50 minutes. You may substitute chopped cooked ham for the chicken, adding 2 teaspoons prepared mustard to the soup mixture. SERVES 8 TO 10

NOTE: Great to take to a new neighbor or a family with a new baby.

Quail Superb

12 quail, cleaned
Salt and pepper to taste
1 onion, sliced
1 cup dry sherry
1/2 cup (1 stick) butter, melted

1/2 cup currant jelly, melted
1 to 2 teaspoons garlic powder
1 tablespoon cornstarch
2 tablespoons cold water

Sprinkle the quail with salt and pepper. Arrange the quail breast side down in a baking pan. Top with the onion slices. Mix the sherry, butter, jelly and garlic powder in a bowl and pour over the quail. Marinate, covered, in the refrigerator for 1 hour, turning occasionally.

   Drain the quail, reserving the marinade. Mix the cornstarch and cold water in a small bowl until blended. Add the reserved marinade to the cornstarch mixture and mix well. Brush the quail with the marinade mixture. Bake at 350 degrees for 45 minutes or until cooked through, basting with the marinade mixture frequently. SERVES 6

Catfish Parmesan

6 pan-dressed skinned catfish fillets
1 cup dry bread crumbs
3/4 cup (3 ounces) grated Parmesan cheese
1/4 cup chopped fresh parsley
2 teaspoons salt
1 teaspoon paprika
1/2 teaspoon basil
1/2 teaspoon pepper
1/2 cup (1 stick) margarine, melted

Pat the fish dry with paper towels. Mix the bread crumbs, cheese, parsley, salt, paprika, basil and pepper in a shallow dish. Dip the fillets into the margarine and coat with the crumb mixture.

Arrange the fillets in a single layer in a greased baking dish. Bake at 375 degrees for 25 minutes or until the fillets flake easily. Garnish with lemon wedges. SERVES 4 TO 6

Pecan-Crusted Salmon

1 (6- to 8-ounce) salmon fillet
1 tablespoon dill mustard
2 tablespoons brown sugar
1/4 cup pecan pieces

Spray the skin side of the fillet with nonstick cooking spray. Spread the dill mustard over the flesh side of the fillet. Sprinkle with the brown sugar and pecan pieces and pat firmly to ensure the pecans adhere.

Arrange the fillet skin side down on a grill rack. Grill over hot coals for 10 to 15 minutes or until the fillet flakes easily; do not turn. SERVES 1

Seared Roasted Salmon with Pineapple Salsa

PINEAPPLE SALSA
1 fresh pineapple, thinly sliced and finely chopped
2 kiwifruit, sliced and chopped
3 green onions, chopped
¼ red or yellow bell pepper, chopped
2 tablespoons chopped fresh cilantro
2 tablespoons brown sugar
Juice of 1 lime

SALMON
4 salmon fillets
Salt and pepper to taste
1 tablespoon Bertolli olive oil

For the salsa, combine the pineapple, kiwifruit, green onions, bell pepper, cilantro, brown sugar and lime juice in a bowl and mix well. Chill, covered, until serving time.

For the salmon, sprinkle the fillets with salt and pepper. Heat the olive oil in a large cast-iron skillet just until the smoking point. Sear the fillets skin side up in the hot olive oil for 1 minute or until brown; turn. Roast at 500 degrees for 4 to 5 minutes for medium-rare or 8 to 10 minutes for medium-well. Serve the fillets topped with salsa. SERVES 4

NOTE: For a real treat, grill the salmon.

There is nothing like the smell of hamburgers on the grill. Grilling and outdoor cooking have become popular, whether the method is charcoal, gas, or even electric. Some grills have added side burners and other features allowing cooks to prepare a whole meal without heating up the kitchen. How do you tell the temperature of an open fire? Hold your hand over the coals at the height the food will be cooked and count how many seconds you can hold your hand in that position before the heat forces you to move. Use the following as a temperature guide.

2 SECONDS/HOT COALS
375+ degrees

3 SECONDS/MEDIUM-HOT COALS
350 to 370 degrees

4 SECONDS/MEDIUM COALS
300 to 350 degrees

5 SECONDS/LOW COALS
200 to 300 degrees

Cajun Creole Crab Cakes

Roasted Pepper and Pineapple Salsa

Heat $1/4$ cup Bertolli extra-virgin olive oil in a skillet over medium heat. Add one 4-ounce jar pimentos, $1 1/2$ cups chopped fresh pineapple, $1/4$ cup lime juice, 2 minced seeded serrano chiles, 2 tablespoons pineapple sage, 2 tablespoons apple jelly, 1 tablespoon chopped fresh cilantro, 1 teaspoon Tabasco sauce and $1/2$ teaspoon pepper to the hot olive oil. Cook just until the jelly melts, stirring frequently. Remove from the heat. Cover to keep warm.

SERVES 6

$1/2$ cup chopped green onions with tops
$1/3$ cup Hellmann's mayonnaise
2 eggs, beaten
1 tablespoon minced fresh parsley
2 teaspoons Worcestershire sauce
2 teaspoons whole-grain mustard
$1/4$ teaspoon cayenne pepper
2 cups seasoned croutons, crumbled
1 pound lump crab meat, shells and cartilage removed
Bertolli olive oil
Roasted Pepper and Pineapple Salsa (sidebar)

Combine the green onions, mayonnaise, eggs, parsley, Worcestershire sauce, mustard, cayenne pepper and $1/2$ of the crouton crumbs in a bowl and mix well. Fold in the crab meat. Shape the crab meat mixture into 6 cakes. You may prepare to this point up to 4 hours in advance and store, covered, in the refrigerator.

Coat the cakes on both sides with the remaining crouton crumbs. Arrange the cakes on a baking sheet lightly coated with olive oil. Bake at 375 degrees for 10 minutes; turn. Bake for 10 to 15 minutes longer or until light brown. Serve with Roasted Pepper and Pineapple Salsa. SERVES 6

Shrimp Mediterranean with Orzo

1 bunch scallions with some of the tops, chopped
1 tablespoon Bertolli olive oil
3 garlic cloves, minced
1 pound shrimp, peeled and deveined
4 plum tomatoes, chopped
4 ounces feta cheese, crumbled
2 eggs, lightly beaten
1/2 cup heavy cream
1 tablespoon chopped fresh dill weed
1/4 teaspoon Tabasco sauce
1/4 teaspoon salt
1/4 teaspoon pepper
8 ounces orzo, cooked and drained

Sauté the scallions in the olive oil in a skillet until tender. Stir in the garlic. Sauté for 1 minute. Spoon the scallion mixture over the bottom of a greased 2- to 2 1/2-quart baking dish. Layer the shrimp, tomatoes and cheese over the prepared layer in the order listed.

Combine the eggs, cream, dill weed, Tabasco sauce, salt and pepper in a bowl and mix well. Pour the egg mixture over the prepared layers. Bake at 400 degrees for 17 minutes. Spoon over hot orzo on dinner plates. SERVES 4

NOTE: Orzo is a rice-shaped pasta.

Shrimp Scampi with Linguini

16 ounces linguini
3 garlic cloves, minced
1/2 cup Bertolli olive oil
8 ounces medium shrimp, peeled, deveined and cut lengthwise into halves
1 teaspoon lemon juice

1/2 teaspoon salt
1/2 teaspoon pepper
1 teaspoon basil, or 1/4 cup chopped fresh basil
1/4 cup chopped fresh Italian parsley
1/8 teaspoon red pepper flakes

Cook the pasta using the package directions. Drain and rinse with hot water. Cover to keep warm. Sauté the garlic in the olive oil in a large skillet. Add the shrimp. Stir-fry until the shrimp turn pink. Drizzle with the lemon juice and sprinkle with salt, pepper, basil, parsley and red pepper flakes.

Spoon the shrimp mixture over the pasta on a serving platter. Sprinkle with Parmesan cheese, if desired. Serve immediately. SERVES 4 TO 6

Szechuan Shrimp

1 pound fresh or thawed frozen shrimp, peeled and deveined
2 tablespoons water
2 tablespoons ketchup
1 tablespoon soy sauce
1 tablespoon rice wine or dry sherry

2 teaspoons cornstarch
1 teaspoon honey
1/2 teaspoon crushed red pepper
1/4 teaspoon ginger
4 garlic cloves, minced
1 tablespoon vegetable oil

Cut the shrimp lengthwise into halves. Combine the water, ketchup, soy sauce, wine, cornstarch, honey, red pepper and ginger in a bowl and mix well.

Stir-fry the garlic in the oil in a large skillet or wok for 30 seconds. Add the shrimp. Stir-fry for 2 to 3 minutes or until the shrimp turn pink; push the shrimp to the side of the skillet. Pour the ketchup mixture into the center of the skillet. Cook until thickened and bubbly, stirring constantly. Cook for 2 minutes longer, stirring constantly. Stir the shrimp into the ketchup mixture. Serve with hot cooked rice and steamed pea pods. SERVES 4

Low-Country Shrimp and Grits

GRITS
1 cup quick-cooking grits
3/4 cup (3 ounces) shredded extra-sharp white Cheddar cheese
1/2 cup (2 ounces) grated Parmesan cheese
1/4 cup (1/2 stick) unsalted butter
1 1/2 teaspoons Tabasco sauce
1 teaspoon cayenne pepper
Salt and pepper to taste

SHRIMP
2 cups chopped smoked bacon
3 tablespoons Bertolli olive oil
1 1/2 pounds (26 to 30 count) shrimp, peeled and deveined
Salt and pepper to taste
1 tablespoon minced garlic
3 cups sliced fresh white mushrooms
3 tablespoons white wine
2 tablespoons lemon juice
2 cups sliced scallions

For the grits, cook the grits using the package directions. Add the Cheddar cheese, Parmesan cheese, butter, Tabasco sauce and cayenne pepper at the end of the cooking process and whisk until incorporated. Season with salt and pepper. Cover to keep warm.

For the shrimp, fry the bacon in a skillet just until it begins to brown. Remove from the heat. Drain, reserving the bacon and 2 tablespoons of the bacon drippings. Heat a large skillet over high heat until hot and add the reserved bacon drippings and olive oil. Heat until the olive oil mixture begins to smoke. Spread the shrimp over the bottom of the hot skillet and sprinkle with salt and pepper before stirring.

Cook until the shrimp begin to turn pink, stirring frequently. Add the reserved bacon and garlic to the shrimp mixture and sauté just until the garlic is tender; be careful not to allow the garlic to burn. Add the mushrooms and toss to coat. Add the wine and lemon juice and mix well. Cook for 30 seconds or until incorporated, stirring constantly. Just before serving, stir in the scallions. Cook for 20 seconds, stirring constantly. The scallions should not be added until just before serving as they tend to lose their crunchy consistency and turn brown if added too far in advance. Spoon the shrimp mixture over the grits on a serving platter. SERVES 4

Shrimp Jambalaya

8 ounces minced cooked ham
1/4 cup bacon drippings or margarine
1 cup chopped yellow onion
1 cup chopped green onions
1 cup chopped green bell pepper
3 garlic cloves, minced
1 teaspoon thyme
2 cups long grain rice
3 to 4 tablespoons tomato paste
8 ounces smoked sausage
2 (16-ounce) cans diced tomatoes
2 cups clam juice or oyster juice
1/2 cup chopped celery
1/4 cup chopped fresh parsley
2 teaspoons salt
1/2 teaspoon pepper
1 bay leaf
Cayenne pepper to taste
3 pounds deveined peeled shrimp

Sauté the ham in the bacon drippings in a skillet for 3 minutes. Stir in the yellow onion, green onions, bell pepper, garlic and thyme. Sauté for 5 minutes. Add the rice and mix well. Cook for 3 minutes, stirring constantly. Stir in the tomato paste and cook for 3 minutes longer, stirring constantly.

Spoon the ham mixture into a stockpot. Add the sausage, undrained tomatoes, clam juice, celery, parsley, salt, pepper, bay leaf and cayenne pepper and mix well. Bring to a boil; reduce the heat. Cook, covered, over low heat for 12 to 15 minutes or until the rice is tender, stirring occasionally. Stir in the shrimp. Cook over low heat for 15 to 20 minutes longer or until the shrimp turn pink, stirring occasionally. Discard the bay leaf. Ladle into bowls. SERVES 4

Desserts

Almond Torte with Raspberry Sauce

RASPBERRY SAUCE
1 (16-ounce) package frozen raspberries, thawed and drained
1/2 cup sugar

TORTE AND ASSEMBLY
7 ounces almond paste
3/4 cup sugar
1/2 cup (1 stick) butter
3 eggs
1/2 cup flour, sifted
1/3 teaspoon baking powder
1 tablespoon amaretto
1/4 teaspoon vanilla extract
Confectioners' sugar

For the sauce, mix the raspberries and sugar in a bowl. Chill, covered, in the refrigerator.

For the torte, combine the almond paste, sugar and butter in a mixing bowl and beat until blended. Add the eggs 1 at a time, mixing well after each addition. Stir in a mixture of the flour and baking powder. Add the liqueur and vanilla and mix well; do not overbeat. Spread in a greased 8-inch baking dish.

Bake at 350 degrees for 40 to 50 minutes or until the edge pulls from the side of the dish. Cool in the pan and cut into 8 wedges. Serve with the sauce and confectioners' sugar. Garnish with fresh raspberries. SERVES 8

NOTE: Soften almond paste by placing in a resealable plastic bag with sliced apples or a couple of slices of fresh bread for 8 to 10 hours.

Amazing Amaretto Cake

CAKE
1/2 cup finely chopped pecans (optional)
Flour
1 (2-layer) package butter recipe yellow cake mix
1 (4-ounce) package white chocolate instant pudding mix
1/2 cup amaretto
1/2 cup water
1/2 cup vegetable oil
4 eggs

AMARETTO GLAZE
1 1/4 cups sugar
1/2 cup (1 stick) butter
1/4 cup amaretto
1/4 cup water
3/4 tablespoon almond extract

For the cake, coat the pecans lightly with flour and sprinkle over the bottom of a greased and floured bundt pan. Combine the cake mix, pudding mix, liqueur, water, oil and eggs in a mixing bowl. Beat for 2 to 3 minutes or until blended, scraping the bowl occasionally. Spoon the batter into the prepared pan. Bake at 325 degrees for 50 to 60 minutes or until the cake tests done.

For the glaze, combine the sugar, butter, liqueur, water and flavoring in a saucepan. Bring to a boil. Boil for 2 minutes or until foamy, stirring occasionally. Poke holes in the hot cake with a wooden pick and pour the hot glaze over the cake. Let stand in the pan for 25 minutes. Invert onto a cake plate. SERVES 16

NOTE: For rum lovers, substitute rum for the amaretto throughout the recipe and omit the white chocolate pudding from the cake batter.

Black Forest Cake

CAKE

2 cups sifted flour
1/4 teaspoon salt
1 1/2 teaspoons baking soda
2/3 cup buttermilk
2 cups sugar

1 cup (2 sticks) butter
4 eggs
1 teaspoon vanilla extract
3 ounces unsweetened chocolate
2/3 cup boiling water

FILLING AND ASSEMBLY

2 (17-ounce) cans pitted dark sweet
  cherries
1/4 cup water
2 tablespoons cornstarch

3 cups whipping cream
1/2 cup confectioners' sugar
2 2/3 tablespoons kirsch

For the cake, sift the flour and salt together. Dissolve the baking soda in the buttermilk in a bowl and stir. Beat the sugar and butter in a mixing bowl until creamy, scraping the bowl occasionally. Add the eggs to the creamed mixture 1 at a time, beating well after each addition. Add the flour mixture and buttermilk mixture alternately to the creamed mixture, beating well after each addition. Add the vanilla and mix well. Melt the chocolate in the water and beat into the creamed mixture.

Spoon the batter into 3 greased and floured 9-inch cake pans. Bake at 325 degrees for 15 to 20 minutes or until the layers test done. Cool in the pans for 10 minutes. Remove to a wire rack to cool completely.

For the filling, drain the cherries, reserving the liquid and cherries. Bring the reserved liquid to a boil in a saucepan over medium heat. Mix the water and cornstarch in a bowl and stir until smooth. Stir the cornstarch mixture into the boiling liquid and mix well.

Cook until clear and thickened, stirring constantly. Remove from the heat. Stir in the cherries. Let stand until cool. Beat the whipping cream in a mixing bowl until soft peaks form. Sprinkle the confectioners' sugar over the whipped cream and beat until firm peaks form. Add 1/2 of the brandy gradually, beating constantly until incorporated.

To assemble, arrange 1 of the cake layers on a cake plate. Spoon alternate rings of the whipped cream mixture and filling over the layer. Layer with another cake layer. Pierce the layer with a fork and brush with the remaining brandy. Again, spoon alternate rings of the remaining whipped cream mixture and remaining filling over the layer. Top with the remaining cake layer. Spread the remaining whipped cream mixture over the top and side of the cake. Garnish with chocolate curls. Chill, covered, until serving time.
SERVES 12

Blueberry Banana Cake

3 cups flour
2 1/2 cups sugar
1 teaspoon baking soda
1/4 teaspoon salt
1 cup vegetable oil
1/2 cup buttermilk

3 eggs, beaten
2 cups mashed ripe bananas
1 cup chopped pecans
1 1/2 teaspoons vanilla extract
1 cup fresh or drained canned
  blueberries

Blend the flour, sugar, baking soda and salt in a bowl. Whisk the oil, buttermilk and eggs in a bowl. Add the oil mixture to the flour mixture and stir just until moistened; do not overmix. Stir in the bananas, pecans and vanilla. Fold in the blueberries.

Spoon the batter into a greased and floured 10-inch tube pan. Bake at 350 degrees for 1 hour and 25 to 30 minutes or until a wooden pick inserted in the center comes out clean. Cool in the pan for 10 minutes. Remove to a wire rack to cool completely.
SERVES 16

Ultimate Chocolate Sin Cake

2 cups sugar
1 3/4 cups flour
3/4 cup baking cocoa
1 1/2 teaspoons baking powder
1 1/2 teaspoons baking soda
1 teaspoon salt
1 cup milk
1/2 cup vegetable oil

2 eggs
2 teaspoons vanilla extract
1 cup boiling water
1 cup (2 sticks) butter, softened
2 cups confectioners' sugar
1 cup baking cocoa
1/3 cup Godiva liqueur or water

Mix the first 6 ingredients in a mixing bowl. Add the milk, oil, eggs and vanilla. Beat at medium speed for 2 minutes, scraping the bowl occasionally. Stir in the boiling water; the batter will be thin. Pour the batter into 2 greased and floured 9-inch cake pans. Bake at 350 degrees for 30 to 35 minutes or until a wooden pick inserted in the center comes out clean. Cool in the pans for 10 minutes. Remove to a wire rack to cool completely.

Beat the butter in a mixing bowl until creamy. Add the confectioners' sugar, baking cocoa and liqueur and beat until smooth. Spread the frosting between the cake layers and over the top and side of the cake. Garnish with fresh strawberries or fresh raspberries. SERVES 12

Black Bottom Cups

An elegant cupcake.

8 ounces cream cheese
1/3 cup sugar
1 egg
1/8 teaspoon salt
1 cup (6 ounces) semisweet chocolate
    chips
1 1/2 cups flour
1 cup sugar

1/4 cup baking cocoa
1 teaspoon baking soda
1/2 teaspoon salt
1 cup water
1/3 cup vegetable oil
1 tablespoon vinegar
1 teaspoon vanilla extract

Beat the cream cheese, 1/3 cup sugar, egg and 1/8 teaspoon salt in a mixing bowl until blended. Stir in the chocolate chips. Sift the flour, 1 cup sugar, baking cocoa, baking soda and 1/2 teaspoon salt into a mixing bowl and mix well. Add the water, oil, vinegar and vanilla and beat until blended.

Fill muffin cups 1/3 full with the chocolate batter and top each with 1 heaping teaspoonful of the cream cheese mixture. Bake at 350 degrees for 30 to 35 minutes. MAKES 2 DOZEN CUPCAKES

Five-Day Coconut Cake

1 (2-layer) package white cake mix
2 cups sugar
2 cups sour cream

1 teaspoon vanilla extract
4 (8-ounce) packages frozen shredded
    coconut

Prepare and bake the cake using the package instructions for two 9-inch cake pans. Cool in the pans for 10 minutes. Remove to a wire rack to cool completely. Split each layer horizontally into halves.

Combine the sugar, sour cream, vanilla and 3 packages of the coconut in a bowl and mix well. Spread the sour cream mixture between the layers and over the top and side of the cake. Sprinkle with the remaining coconut. Chill, covered, in the refrigerator for 5 days before serving. SERVES 12 TO 16

NOTE: This is truly a great dessert for a busy holiday meal since you prepare the cake five days in advance. It frees you up for visiting with family and friends.

Buttery Italian Cream Cake

CAKE

2 cups sugar
2 cups flour
1 teaspoon baking soda
1 teaspoon salt
5 egg whites
1/2 cup shortening
1/2 cup (1 stick) margarine
5 egg yolks

1 teaspoon vanilla butter and nut
  flavoring
1 cup buttermilk
2 cups shredded coconut
1 cup chopped pecans
1/2 cup maraschino cherries, chopped

CREAM CHEESE FROSTING

8 ounces cream cheese, softened
1/2 cup (1 stick) butter, softened
1 (16-ounce) package confectioners'
  sugar

1 teaspoon vanilla butter and nut
  flavoring
1 cup chopped pecans

For the cake, mix the sugar, flour, baking soda and salt in a bowl. Beat the egg whites in a mixing bowl until stiff peaks form; set aside. Cream the shortening and margarine in a mixing bowl until light and fluffy. Add the egg yolks 1 at a time, beating well after each addition. Beat in the flavoring. Add the sugar mixture alternately with the buttermilk, beating well after each addition. Stir in the coconut, pecans and cherries. Fold in the egg whites.

Spoon the batter into 3 round cake pans. Bake at 350 degrees for 30 to 40 minutes or until the layers test done. Cool in the pans for 10 minutes. Remove to a wire rack to cool completely.

For the frosting, beat the cream cheese and butter in a mixing bowl until creamy. Add the confectioners' sugar and flavoring and beat to a spreading consistency. Fold in the pecans. Spread the frosting between the layers and over the top and side of the cake.
SERVES 12

Great Grandmother's Jam Cake with Caramel Frosting

CAKE

2 cups buttermilk
1 1/2 teaspoons baking soda
3 1/2 cups flour
1 teaspoon allspice
1 teaspoon nutmeg
1 teaspoon cinnamon

1 1/2 cups blackberry preserves
1 cup chopped walnuts
1 cup raisins or currants
2 cups sugar
1 cup (2 sticks) butter
4 eggs

CARAMEL FROSTING

2 cups sugar
1/2 cup (1 stick) butter

1/2 cup milk

For the cake, mix the buttermilk and baking soda in a small bowl. Combine the flour, allspice, nutmeg and cinnamon in a bowl and mix well. Stir in the preserves, walnuts and raisins. Beat the sugar and butter in a mixing bowl until light and fluffy, scraping the bowl occasionally. Add the eggs to the butter mixture 1 at a time, beating well after each addition. Stir in the buttermilk mixture. Add the flour mixture gradually, stirring constantly.

Spoon the batter into 3 buttered and floured 9-inch cake pans. Bake at 350 degrees for 30 minutes or until the layers test done. Cool in the pans for 10 minutes. Remove to a wire rack to cool completely.

For the frosting, bring the sugar, butter and milk to a boil in a saucepan, stirring occasionally. Boil for 2 minutes. Let stand until cool. Beat with a wooden spoon to a spreading consistency. Spread the frosting between the layers and over the top and side of the cake. SERVES 12

Lemonade Cake

1 (3-ounce) package lemon gelatin
3/4 cup boiling water
1 (2-layer) package yellow cake mix
1/3 cup vegetable oil
4 eggs
Grated zest of 1 lemon
2 cups confectioners' sugar
1 (6-ounce) can frozen lemonade concentrate

Combine the gelatin and boiling water in a heatproof bowl and stir until the gelatin dissolves. Let stand until cool. Combine the cake mix, oil, eggs, lemon zest and cooled gelatin in a bowl and mix well. Spoon the batter into a 9×13-inch cake pan. Bake at 350 degrees for 30 to 35 minutes or until a wooden pick inserted in the center comes out clean. Cool for 5 minutes.

Pierce the top of the cake with an ice pick. Pour a mixture of the confectioners' sugar and lemonade concentrate over the top of the cake. Garnish with lemon slices.
SERVES 15

White Monarch Cake with Caramel Icing

CAKE
2²/₃ cups flour
1 tablespoon baking powder
¹/₄ teaspoon salt
1 cup (2 sticks) butter
1¹/₂ cups sugar
4 egg whites
1 egg
1 cup ice water
1 teaspoon vanilla extract

CARAMEL ICING
1 (16-ounce) package brown sugar
¹/₂ cup coffee cream
¹/₂ cup (1 stick) margarine

For the cake, mix the flour, baking powder and salt together. Cream the butter and sugar in a mixing bowl. Add the egg whites and egg 1 at a time, beating well after each addition. Add the ice water and vanilla and mix well. Add the flour mixture gradually, beating constantly. Beat at medium-high speed for 2 to 3 minutes, scraping the bowl occasionally. Spoon the batter into two 8-inch cake pans. Bake at 350 degrees for 40 minutes or until the layers test done. Cool in the pans for 10 minutes. Remove to a wire rack to cool completely.

For the icing, combine the brown sugar, coffee cream and margarine in a saucepan. Bring to a rolling boil, stirring occasionally, and boil for 5 to 6 minutes. Let stand until cool. Beat until creamy and spread between the layers and over the top and side of the cake. You may substitute your favorite chocolate icing for the caramel icing. SERVES 12

Poppy Seed Cake

CAKE

1/3 cup poppy seeds
3/4 cup milk
2 cups cake flour
2 1/2 teaspoons baking powder
1/4 teaspoon salt

3/4 cup (1 1/2 sticks) butter
1 1/2 cups sugar
1 1/2 teaspoons vanilla extract
4 egg whites, stiffly beaten

FILLING

1/2 cup sugar
1 tablespoon cornstarch
1 1/2 cups milk
4 egg yolks, lightly beaten

1 teaspoon vanilla extract
1/4 cup chopped walnuts
Confectioners' sugar

For the cake, soak the poppy seeds in the milk in a bowl for 1 hour. Sift the cake flour, baking powder and salt together. Beat the butter in a mixing bowl until creamy. Add the sugar gradually, beating constantly until light and fluffy. Beat in the poppy seed mixture and vanilla. Stir in the flour mixture and fold in the egg whites.

Spoon the batter into 2 greased and lightly floured 8-inch cake pans. Bake at 375 degrees for 20 to 25 minutes or until the layers test done. Cool in the pans for 10 minutes. Remove to a wire rack to cool completely. Cut each layer horizontally into halves.

For the filling, mix the sugar and cornstarch in a saucepan. Whisk the milk and eggs yolks in a bowl until blended. Add the milk mixture to the sugar mixture gradually, stirring constantly. Cook for 1 minute or until the mixture comes to a boil and thickens, stirring constantly. Cool slightly. Stir in the vanilla and walnuts. Spread the filling between the layers. Chill, covered, for 2 to 3 hours. Sift confectioners' sugar over the top of the cake before serving. SERVES 12

Ba-Ba Rum Cake

CAKE
1/2 cup chopped pecans
1 (2-layer) package butter recipe yellow
  cake mix
1/2 cup light rum

1/2 cup water
1/2 cup vegetable oil
4 eggs

RUM GLAZE
1 cup sugar
1/2 cup (1 stick) butter

1/3 cup light rum
1/4 cup water

For the cake, sprinkle the pecans over the bottom of a greased bundt pan. Blend the cake mix, rum, water, oil and eggs in a mixing bowl. Spoon the batter into the prepared pan. Bake at 350 degrees for 45 minutes. Cool in the pan on a wire rack.

  For the glaze, combine the sugar, butter, rum and water in a saucepan. Bring to a boil, stirring occasionally. Boil until the sugar dissolves, stirring occasionally. Release the edge of the cake from the pan using a fork. Pour the hot glaze around the outer edge. Let stand for several minutes and invert the cake onto a cake plate. Brush any dry areas with the glaze. SERVES 16

NOTE: Bake in miniature bundt pans and give to friends during the holidays.

Strawberry Tunnel Cake

1 angel food cake
8 ounces cream cheese, softened
1 (14-ounce) can sweetened
  condensed milk

1/4 cup lemon juice
1 teaspoon almond extract
2 cups sliced strawberries
12 ounces whipped topping

Cut the top 1 inch from the cake and reserve. Hollow out the cake, leaving a 1-inch shell and reserving the cake pieces. Beat the cream cheese in a mixing bowl until creamy. Add the condensed milk, lemon juice and flavoring and beat until blended. Fold in the reserved cake pieces and strawberries.

  Spoon the cream cheese mixture into the shell and replace the top. Chill, covered, for 8 to 10 hours. Spread the top and side of the cake with the whipped topping and garnish as desired. Store, covered, in the refrigerator. SERVES 12

Almond Squares

1 cup (2 sticks) butter
3/4 cup sugar
1 egg yolk
1/2 cup almond paste

1 teaspoon almond extract
2 cups sifted flour
1 egg white
1/4 cup sliced almonds

Beat the butter and sugar in a mixing bowl until light and fluffy. Beat in the egg yolk until blended. Add the almond paste and flavoring and beat until smooth. Add the flour.

Beat at low speed just until combined. Press the dough over the bottom of an ungreased 8×8-inch baking pan. Beat the egg white in a mixing bowl until frothy and brush over the top of the prepared layer. Sprinkle with the almonds. Bake at 350 degrees for 30 minutes or until golden brown. Cool and cut into 1¹/2-inch squares. MAKES 16 SQUARES

Apricot Bars

1 cup (2 sticks) butter
3/4 cup sugar
2 cups flour
1/2 teaspoon baking soda
1/2 teaspoon salt

2/3 cup grated or shredded coconut
1/2 cup chopped pecans
1 (16-ounce) jar apricot preserves
Confectioners' sugar

Beat the butter and sugar in a mixing bowl until creamy. Add a mixture of the flour, baking soda and salt and beat until blended. Stir in the coconut and pecans. Pat 2/3 of the dough in a greased 9×13-inch baking pan. Bake at 350 degrees for 10 minutes.

Remove the baked layer from the oven and immediately spread with the preserves. Top with the remaining dough. Bake for 30 minutes longer. Cool slightly, sprinkle with confectioners' sugar and cut into bars. MAKES 3 TO 4 DOZEN BARS

Banana Crunch Bars

1 3/4 cups chocolate wafer crumbs
  (about 3 dozen wafers)
1/2 cup sugar
1/4 cup baking cocoa
1 teaspoon vanilla extract
1/2 cup (1 stick) butter, melted
3 tablespoons light corn syrup
2 tablespoons butter
2 bananas, sliced
1 teaspoon rum extract
1/2 cup (3 ounces) semisweet chocolate morsels
1/2 cup (3 ounces) peanut butter morsels
1 teaspoon shortening

Mix the wafer crumbs, sugar, baking cocoa and vanilla in a bowl. Stir in 1/2 cup melted butter. Press the crumb mixture over the bottom of a greased 8×8-inch baking pan. Bake at 350 degrees for 10 minutes. Cool for 10 minutes.

Combine the corn syrup and 2 tablespoons butter in a saucepan. Cook over medium heat until the butter melts and the mixture bubbles, stirring frequently. Remove from the heat. Stir in the bananas and flavoring. Spoon evenly over the baked layer.

Combine the chocolate morsels, peanut butter morsels and shortening in a saucepan. Cook over low heat until blended, stirring frequently. Drizzle over the prepared layers. Chill, covered, until set. Let stand at room temperature for 20 minutes and cut into bars.
MAKES 16 TO 20 BARS

Chocolate Mint Sandwich Cookies

1³/4 cups flour
2 teaspoons baking soda
¹/4 teaspoon salt
²/3 cup shortening
¹/2 cup sugar
1 cup (6 ounces) semisweet chocolate
   chips, melted

¹/4 cup light corn syrup
1 egg
³/4 teaspoon peppermint extract
5 to 7 tablespoons sugar
1 bag crème de menthe mints

Mix the flour, baking soda and salt together. Beat the shortening, ¹/2 cup sugar, chocolate chips, corn syrup, egg and flavoring in a mixing bowl until creamy, scraping the bowl occasionally. Add the flour mixture and beat until blended. Shape the dough into quarter-size balls and roll in 5 to 7 tablespoons sugar.

Arrange the balls on a greased cookie sheet. Bake at 350 degrees for 10 minutes. Cool on the cookie sheet for 2 minutes. Turn ¹/2 of the cookies and place 1 mint on each. Top with the remaining warm cookies and press lightly, helping the mints to melt and drizzle out the side of the cookie sandwiches. MAKES 1¹/2 TO 2 DOZEN COOKIES

NOTE: Make these in advance and freeze. Thaw at room temperature.

Grandma's Cornflake Cookies

2 cups sifted flour
1 teaspoon baking soda
¹/2 teaspoon salt
¹/2 teaspoon baking powder
1¹/4 cups shortening
1 cup sugar

1 cup packed brown sugar
2 eggs, beaten
1 teaspoon vanilla extract
2 cups shredded coconut
2 cups cornflakes

Sift the flour, baking soda, salt and baking powder together. Beat the shortening, sugar and brown sugar in a mixing bowl until creamy. Add the eggs and vanilla and beat until blended. Add the flour mixture and beat until smooth. Stir in the coconut and cornflakes.

Drop the batter by spoonfuls 1¹/2 inches apart on a greased cookie sheet. Bake at 350 degrees for 8 to 10 minutes or until light brown. Cool on the cookie sheet for 2 minutes. Remove to a wire rack to cool completely. MAKES 3¹/2 DOZEN COOKIES

Crunch Drops

2 cups sifted flour
1 teaspoon baking soda
1/2 teaspoon salt
1 cup shortening
1 cup sugar
1 cup packed brown
  sugar

2 eggs
1 teaspoon vanilla extract
2 cups quick-cooking oats
2 cups crisp rice cereal
1 cup shredded fresh,
  canned or packaged
  coconut

Sift the flour, baking soda and salt together. Beat the shortening in a mixing bowl until light and fluffy. Add the sugar and brown sugar and beat until smooth and creamy. Add the eggs 1 at a time, beating well after each addition. Stir in the vanilla and flour mixture. Add the oats, cereal and coconut and mix well; the dough will be very stiff.

Drop by teaspoonfuls onto a greased cookie sheet. Bake at 350 degrees for 12 to 15 minutes or until light brown. Cool on the cookie sheet for 2 minutes. Remove to a wire rack to cool completely.
MAKES 5 DOZEN COOKIES

SENATOR WENDELL AND JEAN FORD

Senator Wendell Hampton Ford, a native of Owensboro, served thirty-three years in state and national politics. Ford served first as governor of Kentucky, then as a United States senator. His twenty-four-year term as senator stands as the longest term of any United States senator from Kentucky. Ford's motto reflects his dedication to Kentucky and to his hometown of Owensboro—"The only reason for the existence of government at any level is to serve people." Senator and Jean Ford requested Crunch Drops (at left) for many teas and gatherings at the Old Mansion in Frankfort.

Molasses Cookies

1 cup sugar
3/4 cup shortening
1/4 cup molasses
1 egg, beaten
2 teaspoons baking soda
1 teaspoon ground cloves

1 teaspoon cinnamon
1 teaspoon ginger
1/2 teaspoon salt
2 cups flour
Sugar to taste

Beat 1 cup sugar, the shortening, molasses and egg in a mixing bowl until creamy. Add the baking soda, cloves, cinnamon, ginger and salt and beat until blended. Add the flour gradually, beating constantly until smooth. Shape the dough into 1-inch balls.

Dip the top of each ball in sugar to taste and arrange sugar side up on a cookie sheet. Bake at 350 degrees for 8 to 10 minutes or until crisp around the edges. Cool on the cookie sheet for 2 minutes. Remove to a wire rack to cool completely.
MAKES 2 TO 3 DOZEN COOKIES

Caramel Oat Squares

2 cups flour
2 cups quick-cooking oats
1 1/2 cups packed light brown sugar
1 teaspoon baking soda
1/2 teaspoon salt
1 1/4 cups (2 1/2 sticks) margarine, softened

1 cup (6 ounces) semisweet chocolate chips
1/2 cup chopped pecans
1 (12-ounce) jar caramel ice cream topping
3 tablespoons flour

Combine 2 cups flour, the oats, brown sugar, baking soda and salt in a bowl and mix well. Add the margarine and mix until crumbly. Pat 1/2 of the crumb mixture over the bottom of a 9x13-inch baking dish sprayed with nonstick cooking spray. Bake at 350 degrees for 10 minutes. Maintain the oven temperature.

Sprinkle the chocolate chips and pecans over the baked layer. Mix the ice cream topping and 3 tablespoons flour in a bowl and drizzle over the prepared layers. Top with the remaining crumb mixture and pat gently. Bake for 22 minutes longer or until golden brown. Let stand until cool. Cut into 1 1/2-inch squares. MAKES 50 SQUARES

Oatmeal Crispies

COOKIES

1 1/2 cups sifted flour
1 teaspoon salt
1 teaspoon baking soda
1 cup shortening
1 cup packed brown sugar
1 cup sugar
2 eggs, beaten
1 teaspoon vanilla extract
3 cups quick-cooking oats
1/2 cup chopped nuts

CONFECTIONERS' SUGAR GLAZE

1/2 cup confectioners' sugar
1 tablespoon milk

For the cookies, mix the flour, salt and baking soda together. Beat the shortening, brown sugar, sugar, eggs and vanilla in a mixing bowl until creamy. Add the flour mixture, oats and nuts and mix well.

Divide the dough into 2 equal portions and shape each portion into a log. Wrap the logs individually in waxed paper. Chill for 1 hour. Slice each log into 1/4-inch slices and arrange the slices on a cookie sheet. Bake on the middle oven rack at 350 degrees for 10 minutes. Cool on the cookie sheet for 2 minutes. Remove to a wire rack to cool completely.

For the glaze, combine the confectioners' sugar and milk in a bowl and stir until of a glaze consistency. Drizzle the glaze over the cookies. Let stand until set.
MAKES 3 DOZEN COOKIES

NOTE: You may freeze these cookies for up to one month. Bring to room temperature before serving.

Pumpkin Cheesecake Bars

CRUST
1 (16-ounce) package pound cake mix
1 egg
2 tablespoons butter or margarine, melted
2 teaspoons pumpkin pie spice

PUMPKIN FILLING
8 ounces cream cheese, softened
1 (14-ounce) can sweetened condensed milk
1 (16-ounce) can solid-pack pumpkin
2 eggs
2 teaspoons pumpkin pie spice
1/2 teaspoon salt
1 cup chopped nuts

For the crust, combine the cake mix, egg, butter and pie spice in a mixing bowl. Beat at low speed until crumbly. Press the crumb mixture over the bottom of a 10×15-inch baking pan.

For the filling, beat the cream cheese in a mixing bowl until light and fluffy. Add the condensed milk gradually, beating constantly until blended. Add the pumpkin, eggs, pie spice and salt and mix well. Spoon the pumpkin mixture over the prepared layer and sprinkle with the nuts. Bake at 350 degrees for 30 to 35 minutes. Cool in the pan on a wire rack. Chill and cut into bars. MAKES 4 DOZEN BARS

Tea Cakes

2 cups flour
1 teaspoon baking powder
1 teaspoon baking soda
1/8 teaspoon salt
1 cup butter-flavor shortening
1 1/2 cups sugar
2 eggs
1 teaspoon vanilla or lemon extract or both

Sift the flour, baking powder, baking soda and salt together. Beat the shortening, sugar and eggs in a mixing bowl until creamy. Beat in the vanilla until blended. Add the flour mixture and mix well.

Shape the dough into 1-inch balls and arrange on a cookie sheet. Bake at 350 degrees for 10 to 12 minutes or until light brown. Cool on the cookie sheet.

MAKES 30 TEA CAKES

Mom's Hot Fudge Sauce

Bring 1 cup sugar, one 5-ounce can evaporated milk, 3 tablespoons baking cocoa, 2 tablespoons flour and 1/4 teaspoon salt to a boil in a saucepan, stirring constantly. Boil for 1 minute. Remove from the heat. Add 1 tablespoon butter and 1 teaspoon vanilla extract and stir until the butter melts. Serve warm as a dipping sauce for fruit or drizzle over warm biscuits.

MAKES ABOUT
1 1/2 CUPS

Almond Apple Pie

1 (2-crust) package refrigerator pie
  pastry
3/4 cup packed brown sugar
3/4 cup sugar
1/4 cup flour
1 teaspoon cinnamon

1/4 teaspoon nutmeg
9 cups thinly sliced peeled apples
1/2 teaspoon almond extract
2/3 cup sliced almonds
3 tablespoons butter

Fit 1 of the pie pastries in a 9-inch pie plate. Mix the brown sugar, sugar, flour, cinnamon and nutmeg in a bowl. Add the apples to the brown sugar mixture and toss to coat. Spoon the apple mixture into the pastry-lined pie plate. Drizzle with the flavoring and sprinkle with the almonds. Dot with the butter. Top with the remaining pastry, fluting the edge and cutting vents.

  Bake at 375 degrees for 40 to 60 minutes or until golden brown, covering the edge with foil 15 to 20 minutes before the end of the baking process to prevent overbrowning. Serve warm with whipped topping or ice cream. SERVES 8

Caramel Crunch Apple Pie

28 caramels
2 tablespoons water
4 cooking apples, peeled and thinly
  sliced
1 unbaked (9-inch) pie shell

3/4 cup flour
1/3 cup sugar
1/2 teaspoon cinnamon
1/3 cup butter or margarine
1/2 cup chopped walnuts

Combine the caramels and water in a double boiler over boiling water. Reduce the heat to low. Cook until blended, stirring occasionally. Place 1/2 of the apples in the pie shell and drizzle with 1/2 of the caramel mixture. Top with the remaining apples and remaining caramel mixture.

  Combine the flour, sugar and cinnamon in a bowl and mix well. Cut the butter into the flour mixture until crumbly. Stir in the walnuts. Sprinkle the crumb mixture over the prepared layers. Bake at 375 degrees for 40 to 45 minutes or until light brown and bubbly. Serve warm. SERVES 6 TO 8

Glazed Apple Pie

PIE
2 homemade pie pastries
1 1/2 cups cornflakes
6 cups thinly sliced tart apples
1 cup sugar
1 teaspoon cinnamon
1 egg white, beaten

GLAZE
1/2 cup confectioners' sugar
3 tablespoons maple syrup

For the pie, fit 1 of the pastries in a 9-inch pie plate. Sprinkle the cereal over the pastry and top with the apples. Sprinkle with the sugar and cinnamon. Top with the remaining pastry, fluting the edge and cutting vents. Brush the pastry with the egg white.

Place the pie plate on a baking sheet. Bake at 350 degrees for 45 to 55 minutes or until the apples are tender and the pastry is golden brown.

For the glaze, mix the confectioners' sugar and syrup in a bowl and drizzle over the warm pie. SERVES 6 TO 8

NOTE: Save time by substituting commercially prepared refrigerator pie pastry for the homemade pastry.

Blueberry Lemon Soufflé Pie

3 cups blueberries
6 tablespoons sugar
3 egg yolks
1/4 cup superfine sugar
1/2 cup plus 3 tablespoons fresh lemon juice
Grated zest of 2 lemons
3 egg whites
1/8 teaspoon salt
3 tablespoons superfine sugar
1 baked (9-inch) pie shell

Toss the blueberries with 6 tablespoons sugar in a nonreactive saucepan. Cook over medium heat for 3 to 5 minutes, stirring frequently. Remove from the heat. Place a strainer over a bowl and pour the blueberry mixture into the strainer. Drain, reserving the blueberries and juices.

Beat the egg yolks with 1/4 cup superfine sugar in a mixing bowl for 2 minutes or until thickened and pale yellow in color. Add the lemon juice gradually, beating constantly until blended. Beat in the lemon zest. Spoon the lemon mixture into a saucepan.

Cook over low heat for 8 minutes or until thickened, stirring frequently. Pour into a bowl. Let stand until cool. Beat the egg whites in a mixing bowl until foamy. Add the salt and beat until soft peaks form. Add 3 tablespoons superfine sugar 1 1/2 teaspoons at a time, beating well after each addition. Stir 1/4 of the egg white mixture into the egg yolk mixture. Fold the remaining egg white mixture 1/3 at a time into the egg yolk mixture.

Spoon the blueberries into the pie shell and drizzle with the reserved juices. Mound the lemon soufflé mixture over the blueberries, spreading to the edge. Bake at 400 degrees for 15 minutes or until light brown. SERVES 12

Chocolate Truffle Pie

1/2 cup pecans pieces, toasted and
   chopped
1 (9-inch) chocolate cookie crumb
   pie shell
25 caramels

1/3 cup evaporated milk
1 1/2 cups (9 ounces) semisweet
   chocolate chips
1 cup heavy cream
3 tablespoons butter or margarine

Spread the pecans over the bottom of the pie shell. Heat the caramels and evaporated milk in a saucepan until blended, stirring frequently. Pour the caramel mixture over the pecans. Heat the chocolate chips, cream and butter in a saucepan until blended, stirring frequently. Pour the chocolate mixture over the prepared layers. Chill, covered, for 4 hours or until set. Garnish with whipped cream. SERVES 6 TO 8

Chocolate Pie

3 eggs
2 cups sugar
1/4 cup flour
3 tablespoons baking cocoa
2 cups milk or half-and-half

1 (9-inch) graham cracker pie shell
6 tablespoons sugar
1/2 teaspoon vanilla extract
1/4 teaspoon salt

Separate the eggs and allow the egg whites to come to room temperature. Combine the egg yolks, 2 cups sugar, flour, baking cocoa and milk in a saucepan. Bring to a boil, stirring frequently. Cook for 10 to 12 minutes or until thickened, stirring constantly. Spoon the chocolate mixture into the pie shell.

   Beat the egg whites in a mixing bowl until stiff peaks form. Add 6 tablespoons sugar, the vanilla and salt and beat until blended. Spread the meringue over the prepared layer, sealing to the edge. Bake at 350 degrees for 12 minutes. SERVES 8

Mother's Flaky Pie Pastry

Mix 4 cups flour, 2 teaspoons salt and 1 tablespoon sugar in a bowl. Cut 1¾ cups shortening into the flour mixture until crumbly. Whisk ½ cup water, 1 tablespoon white vinegar and 1 egg in a bowl until blended. Stir the vinegar mixture into the flour mixture. Chill for 30 minutes. Divide the dough into 5 equal portions and wrap individually in waxed paper. Freeze until needed.

EACH PORTION MAKES 1 PIE PASTRY

Macaroon Pie

1 cup graham cracker crumbs
½ cup chopped nuts
½ cup shredded coconut

4 egg whites
1 cup sugar
Vanilla ice cream

Mix the graham cracker crumbs, nuts and coconut in a bowl. Beat the egg whites and sugar in a mixing bowl until stiff peaks form. Fold the crumb mixture into the meringue.

Press the meringue mixture into a 9-inch pie pan. Bake at 300 degrees for 25 minutes. Top with a layer of vanilla ice cream. SERVES 6 TO 8

Oatmeal Pie

½ cup (1 stick) butter
1 cup milk
¾ cup light corn syrup
1 teaspoon vanilla extract
2 eggs, lightly beaten
¾ cup quick-cooking oats
½ cup sugar

½ cup packed brown sugar
1 cup shredded coconut
1 unbaked (9-inch) pie shell
Chopped pecans

Heat the butter in a saucepan until melted. Stir in the milk, corn syrup, vanilla and eggs. Add the oats, sugar, brown sugar and coconut and mix well. Spoon the oats mixture into the pie shell and sprinkle with pecans.

Bake at 425 degrees for 10 minutes; reduce the oven temperature to 375 degrees. Bake for 25 minutes longer. Do not overbake. SERVES 10 TO 12

Strawberry Chiffon Pie

1 envelope unflavored gelatin
1/3 cup cold water
3/4 to 1 cup sugar
3 egg yolks, lightly beaten
3 tablespoons lemon juice

1/8 teaspoon salt
2 1/2 cups crushed fresh strawberries,
  drained
1 cup whipping cream
1 baked (9-inch) pie shell

Mix the gelatin with the cold water in a measuring cup. Let stand for 1 minute. Combine the gelatin mixture, sugar, egg yolks, lemon juice and salt in a saucepan. Cook over medium heat just until the mixture comes to a boil, stirring constantly. Remove from the heat. Combine the gelatin mixture and strawberries in a bowl and mix gently. Chill for 2 to 3 hours or until the mixture peaks when spooned, stirring occasionally.

Beat the whipping cream in a mixing bowl until soft peaks form. Fold into the strawberry mixture. Spoon the strawberry mixture into the pie shell. Chill, covered, for 4 hours or until set. Garnish with whole strawberries and mint leaves. SERVES 8

NOTE: Light and delicious! Especially good with fresh berries from Reid's Orchard.

Ladyfinger Cheesecake

2 (11-ounce) packages no-bake
  cheesecake mix
2/3 cup butter or margarine, melted
1/4 cup sugar
1 (3-ounce) package ladyfingers
  (25 cookies)

8 ounces cream cheese, softened
3 cups milk
12 ounces frozen whipped topping,
  thawed
1 (21-ounce) can raspberry pie filling or
  flavor of choice

Combine the cheesecake crust mix, butter and sugar in a bowl and stir until crumbly. Press the crumb mixture over the bottom of an ungreased 10-inch springform pan. Arrange the ladyfingers around the edge of the pan.

Beat the cream cheese and 1/2 cup of the milk in a mixing bowl until smooth. Add the remaining 2 1/2 cups milk gradually, beating well after each addition. Add the contents of the cheesecake filling mix to the cream cheese mixture and beat until smooth. Beat at medium speed for 3 minutes longer, scraping the bowl occasionally. Fold in the whipped topping. Spoon the cream cheese mixture over the prepared layer. Chill, covered, for 1 hour or longer. Spread with the pie filling. Remove the sides of the pan before serving. SERVES 10

Peanut Butter Cheesecake

CRUST

1 1/2 cups crushed pretzels

1/3 cup butter, melted

PEANUT BUTTER FILLING

40 ounces cream cheese, softened

1 1/2 cups sugar

3/4 cup creamy peanut butter

2 teaspoons vanilla extract

3 eggs

1 cup (6 ounces) semisweet chocolate chips

1 cup (6 ounces) peanut butter chips

TOPPING

1 cup sour cream

1/2 cup sugar

3 tablespoons creamy peanut butter

1/2 cup finely chopped unsalted peanuts

For the crust, combine the crushed pretzels and butter in a bowl and mix well. Press the crumb mixture over the bottom and 1 inch up the side of a greased 10-inch springform pan. Bake at 350 degrees for 5 minutes. Let stand until cool. Maintain the oven temperature.

For the filling, beat the cream cheese and sugar in a mixing bowl until smooth. Add the peanut butter and vanilla and beat until blended. Add the eggs and beat at low speed just until combined. Stir in the chocolate chips and peanut butter chips. Spread the filling over the baked layer. Bake for 50 to 55 minutes or until the center is almost set. Cool for 15 minutes. Maintain the oven temperature.

For the topping, combine the sour cream, sugar and peanut butter in a bowl and mix well. Spread the topping over the baked layers and sprinkle with the peanuts. Bake for 5 minutes longer. Cool in the pan on a wire rack for 10 minutes. Run a sharp knife around the edge of the pan to loosen the cheesecake. Cool for 1 hour longer. Chill, covered, for 8 to 10 hours. Remove the sides of the pan before serving. SERVES 14

Peach Cranberry Crisp

2 (21-ounce) cans peach pie filling
$^1/_2$ cup fresh or frozen cranberries, chopped
$^1/_2$ cup flour
$^1/_3$ cup packed light brown sugar

$^1/_4$ cup quick-cooking oats
$^1/_4$ cup ($^1/_2$ stick) butter or margarine, softened
$^1/_4$ cup sliced blanched almonds

Mix the pie filling and cranberries in a bowl. Spoon the cranberry mixture into a greased 9×9-inch baking pan. Combine the flour, brown sugar and oats in a bowl and mix well.

Cut the butter into the flour mixture until crumbly. Sprinkle the crumb mixture over the prepared layer and top with the almonds. Bake at 375 degrees for 30 to 40 minutes or until golden brown. SERVES 8

Pumpkin Pie Crunch

1 (16-ounce) can solid-pack pumpkin
1 (12-ounce) can evaporated milk
1$^1/_2$ cups sugar
3 eggs, lightly beaten

4 teaspoons pumpkin pie spice
$^1/_2$ teaspoon salt
1 (2-layer) package yellow cake mix
1 cup (2 sticks) butter, melted

Grease the bottom of a 9×13-inch baking pan. Combine the pumpkin, evaporated milk, sugar, eggs, pie spice and salt in a bowl and mix well. Spoon the pumpkin mixture into the prepared pan.

Sprinkle the cake mix evenly over the top of the prepared layer and drizzle with the butter. Bake at 350 degrees for 50 to 55 minutes or until golden brown. Let stand until cool. Garnish with whipped topping and chopped pecans. Store in the refrigerator. SERVES 15

Chocolate Pâté

PÂTÉ

1/2 cup heavy cream
3 egg yolks
16 ounces semisweet chocolate, broken
1/2 cup light corn syrup

1/2 cup (1 stick) margarine
1 1/2 cups whipping cream
1/4 cup confectioners' sugar
1 teaspoon vanilla extract

RASPBERRY SAUCE

1 (10-ounce) package frozen raspberries, thawed
1/3 cup light corn syrup

For the pâté, whisk the heavy cream and egg yolks in a bowl until blended. Combine the chocolate, corn syrup and margarine in a saucepan. Heat until blended, stirring frequently. Add the egg yolk mixture to the chocolate mixture and mix well. Cook for 3 minutes, stirring frequently. Cool to room temperature.

Beat the whipping cream in a mixing bowl until soft peaks form. Add the confectioners' sugar and vanilla and beat until blended. Fold the whipped cream into the chocolate mixture until combined. Spoon into a 5×9-inch loaf pan lined with plastic wrap. Chill for 3 hours or longer.

For the sauce, process the undrained raspberries in a blender until puréed. Combine the purée and corn syrup in a bowl and mix well. Slice the pâté and serve with the sauce. SERVES 12

Espresso Chocolate Mousse

A chocolate lover's dream come true!

1 cup (6 ounces) chocolate chips
2 eggs
3 tablespoons espresso

1 to 2 tablespoons crème de cacao
3/4 cup milk, scalded
Whipped topping (optional)

Combine the chocolate chips, eggs, espresso and liqueur in a blender. Process for 2 minutes. Add the milk. Process until blended.

Pour the chocolate mixture into 4 goblets. Chill, covered, for 3 hours or until set. Top each serving with a dollop of whipped topping. SERVES 4

Summer Pudding

1 pint fresh strawberries
1 pint fresh blueberries
1 pint fresh blackberries
1 pint fresh raspberries

1 cup sugar
6 slices brioche, egg bread, sourdough
    bread or pound cake
Cinnamon to taste

Toss the strawberries, blueberries, blackberries, raspberries and sugar in a saucepan. Heat until the sugar melts, stirring frequently. Remove from the heat. Cool completely. Spoon 1/3 of the berry mixture into a 9×13-inch dish. Arrange 3 slices of the bread over the fruit and sprinkle lightly with cinnamon. Spoon 1/2 of the remaining berry mixture over the bread and layer with the remaining 3 slices of bread. Top with the remaining berry mixture.

Cover tightly with plastic wrap and press lightly to compact. Chill for 6 hours or longer. Cut into squares and garnish with whipped topping, additional fresh berries and mint leaves. You may prepare up to 2 days in advance and store, covered, in the refrigerator. SERVES 8 TO 10

Melon Balls Melba

1 cup fresh or drained frozen raspberries
3 tablespoons rum
2 tablespoons sugar
1 tablespoon chopped fresh mint
4 cups watermelon balls, or a mixture of watermelon balls and honeydew balls
Sections of 1 navel orange

Press the raspberries through a sieve to purée or process in a food processor until puréed. Combine the purée, rum, sugar and mint in a bowl and mix well. Add the watermelon and mix gently. Chill, covered, for several hours. Add the orange sections to the watermelon mixture and toss to mix. Serve garnished with additional fresh mint. SERVES 6

Winter Fruit Mélange

3 cups thinly sliced peeled fresh pears
1 cup fresh cranberries
2 tart apples, peeled and thinly sliced
Sections of 1 orange
1 (3-inch) cinnamon stick
6 whole cloves
1/2 cup light corn syrup

Arrange the sliced pears, cranberries, sliced apples, orange sections, cinnamon stick and cloves in a decorative pattern in a shallow 2-quart baking dish. Drizzle the corn syrup over the top.

Bake, covered, at 350 degrees for 1 hour or until the pears are tender. Discard the cinnamon stick and cloves. Chill, covered, until serving time. Serve cold or at room temperature. SERVES 8 TO 10

Caribbean Sorbet

2 cups water
1/2 cup sugar
1/2 cup fresh lime juice
Grated zest of 1/2 lime
1 ripe papaya, peeled and sliced

Combine 1 cup of the water and the sugar in a heavy saucepan. Cook over medium heat until the sugar dissolves, stirring occasionally. Remove from the heat and stir in the remaining 1 cup water, lime juice and 3/4 of the lime zest. Chill, covered, in the refrigerator.

Pour the lime mixture into an ice cream freezer container. Freeze using the manufacturer's directions. Spoon the sorbet over the sliced papaya in bowls and sprinkle with the remaining lime zest. MAKES 1 1/2 PINTS

Very Vanilla Ice Cream

1 cup confectioners' sugar
1/2 cup heavy cream
1 tablespoon plus 1 teaspoon vanilla extract
1 quart half-and-half

Combine the confectioners' sugar, heavy cream and vanilla in a bowl and mix until smooth. Stir in the half-and-half. Pour the cream mixture into a freezer container. Freeze using the manufacturer's directions. Serve with your favorite ice cream topping. MAKES 2 QUARTS

Amber Sauce

1 cup packed brown sugar
1/2 cup evaporated milk
1/2 cup light corn syrup
1/4 cup (1/2 stick) butter, softened

Combine the brown sugar, evaporated milk, corn syrup and butter in a saucepan. Cook over low heat for 10 minutes or until blended, stirring frequently. Serve warm over chocolate cake or ice cream. Store, covered, in the refrigerator. MAKES 2 CUPS

Praline Sauce

1 cup light corn syrup
1/2 cup sugar
1/3 cup margarine
1 egg, lightly beaten
1 cup chopped pecans
1 teaspoon vanilla extract

Combine the corn syrup, sugar, margarine and egg in a saucepan. Bring to a boil over medium heat, stirring constantly. Boil for 2 minutes; do not stir. Remove from the heat. Stir in the pecans and vanilla. Serve warm over ice cream, pound cake or angel food cake. Store, covered, in the refrigerator. MAKES 2 CUPS

Just for Kids

Puppy Chow

2 cups chocolate chips
1 cup (2 sticks) butter or margarine
1 cup peanut butter
16 cups Crispix
4 cups confectioners' sugar

Combine the chocolate chips, butter and peanut butter in a microwave-safe dish. Microwave until melted and stir. Combine the chocolate chip mixture and cereal in a large bowl and mix well. Add the confectioners' sugar to the cereal mixture and toss to coat. SERVES 16

JON AND KATIE
BRENNAN

Dogs have always played an important role in Jon and Katie Brennan's family. As an eight-year-old, Katie asked her parents for a sister and received a dog that she named Sister. Jon and Katie have always supported each other's singing careers. Both grew up singing at church, and in 1992, Jon received a part on TV as a member of the cast of MTV's "The Real World." Currently, both Brennans participate in Goldie Payne's show at the Best Little Opry House in Kentucky.

Just for Kids

161

Chocolate Popcorn

Enjoy this snack when viewing movies.

1 cup sugar
3 tablespoons baking cocoa
¹/2 cup light corn syrup
3 tablespoons margarine
2 large bowls popcorn

Mix the sugar and baking cocoa in a saucepan. Stir in the corn syrup and margarine. Cook over medium heat until the mixture begins to boil, stirring occasionally. Boil for 3 to 5 minutes; do not stir. Pour the syrup mixture over the popcorn in a large bowl and toss to coat. MAKES A VARIABLE AMOUNT

White Christmas Snack Mix

2 cups crisp rice cereal
2 cups broken cinnamon graham crackers
2 cups pretzel sticks
2 cups broken caramel rice cakes
1 cup whole cashews
1 pound white chocolate baking pieces, chopped
¹/3 cup heavy cream
1 tablespoon light corn syrup
¹/2 teaspoon almond extract

Toss the cereal, graham crackers, pretzel sticks, rice cakes and cashews in a large bowl. Combine the white chocolate, cream and corn syrup in a saucepan. Cook over low heat until blended, stirring frequently. Remove from the heat and stir gently until smooth. Stir in the flavoring.

Drizzle the warm white chocolate mixture over the cereal mixture and toss gently to coat. Immediately spread the cereal mixture on a baking sheet lined with waxed paper. Let stand for 1 hour or until set. Store in resealable plastic bags. MAKES 14 TO 16 CUPS

Peanut Butter Apple Dip

8 ounces cream cheese, softened
1 cup peanut butter
1 cup packed brown sugar
$1/4$ cup milk
4 apples, cut into wedges

Beat the cream cheese, peanut butter, brown sugar and milk in a mixing bowl until smooth, scraping the bowl occasionally. Serve with the apple wedges. Store leftovers in the refrigerator. MAKES $2^2/3$ CUPS

Jack-O'-Lantern Cheese Ball

10 ounces sharp Cheddar cheese, shredded
1 (8-ounce) can crushed pineapple, drained
8 ounces cream cheese, softened
$1/4$ teaspoon Tabasco sauce
1 (2-inch) rib celery
Pitted black olives

Combine the Cheddar cheese, pineapple, cream cheese and Tabasco sauce in a bowl and mix well. Chill, covered, for 1 hour or until slightly firm. Shape the cheese mixture into a slightly flattened ball and arrange on a serving plate.

Push the celery into the top of the ball to resemble the stem. Slice the olives and press into the ball to form the eyes, nose and mouth. Chill, covered, until serving time. Serve with assorted party crackers. SERVES 12 TO 15

Veggie Pizza

2 cups sour cream
1 envelope ranch dip mix
2 (8-count) cans crescent rolls
1/2 cup finely chopped cauliflower
1/2 cup finely chopped broccoli

1/2 cup finely chopped carrots
1/2 cup finely chopped celery
1 cup (4 ounces) shredded Cheddar
   cheese

Mix the sour cream and dip mix in a bowl. Chill, covered, for 2 hours. Unroll the crescent roll dough and separate into rectangles. Pat over the bottom and up the side of a baking sheet. Bake at 375 degrees for 10 to 15 minutes or until light brown. Let stand until cool.

   Spread the sour cream mixture over the baked layer. Sprinkle with the cauliflower, broccoli, carrots and celery and top with the cheese. Cut into bite-size squares.
SERVES 12

French Toast Dippers

4 or 5 slices white bread
3 cups crisp rice cereal
1 tablespoon sugar
3/4 teaspoon cinnamon
3 eggs

1/2 cup milk
1 teaspoon vanilla extract
1/8 teaspoon salt
2 tablespoons butter, melted

Cut each bread slice crosswise into 4 strips. Arrange the bread strips on a rack. Let stand for 20 minutes to dry out slightly. Place the cereal in a resealable plastic bag and seal tightly. Crush until fine crumbs. Mix the cereal crumbs, sugar and cinnamon in a shallow dish.

   Whisk the eggs, milk, vanilla and salt in a bowl until blended. Dip the bread strips 1 at a time into the egg mixture and coat with the crumb mixture. Arrange the strips in a single layer in a 9×13-inch baking dish and drizzle with the butter. Bake at 425 degrees for 17 to 19 minutes or until hot and crisp. Serve with maple syrup.
SERVES 4 TO 5

Peanut Butter Roll-Ups

12 slices white bread
^{1}/4 cup creamy peanut butter
^{1}/4 cup sugar
2 tablespoons cinnamon
2 tablespoons butter, melted

Trim the crusts from the bread slices and reserve for another use. Roll the bread slices ^{1}/8 inch thick on a hard surface with a rolling pin. Spread 1 teaspoon of the peanut butter on 1 side of each slice.

Mix the sugar and cinnamon in a bowl and sprinkle evenly over the peanut butter. Roll the slices to enclose the filling. Arrange seam side down on a lightly greased baking sheet and brush with the butter. You may freeze at this point for future use. Bake at 350 degrees for 7 minutes per side or until light brown. MAKES 1 DOZEN ROLL-UPS

Dogs in a Sweater

1 (11-ounce) can refrigerator breadsticks
8 popsicle sticks
8 frankfurters

Separate the dough. Roll each into a 15-inch rope. Insert 1 popsicle stick lengthwise into each frankfurter. Starting at 1 end, wrap the dough ropes in a spiral around the frankfurters and pinch the ends to seal.

Arrange the wrapped frankfurters 1 inch apart on a baking sheet coated with nonstick cooking spray. Bake at 350 degrees for 18 to 20 minutes or until light brown. Serve with ketchup, mustard, ranch dressing and/or your favorite toppings. SERVES 8

Ham Puffs

6 cups chopped or ground ham
1/3 cup minced or chopped onion
1 1/2 cups (6 ounces) shredded Swiss cheese
4 eggs, lightly beaten
1 1/2 tablespoons Dijon mustard
1/2 teaspoon pepper
3 (8-count) cans crescent rolls

Combine the ham, onion, cheese, eggs, Dijon mustard and pepper in a bowl and mix well. Unroll 1 can of the crescent roll dough. Roll 1/4 inch thick on a hard surface and cut into 48 squares. Press the squares over the bottom and up the sides of miniature muffin cups. Fill each pastry-lined muffin cup with some of the ham mixture.

   Repeat the process with the remaining crescent roll dough and remaining ham mixture. Bake at 350 degrees for 10 minutes. You may freeze for future use.
MAKES 144 PUFFS

Turkey Tortilla Wheels

2/3 cup soft cream cheese with garden vegetables
2 (10-inch) flour tortillas
6 slices thinly sliced cooked turkey
6 slices mozzarella cheese
1 carrot, peeled and shredded

Spread 1/3 cup of the cream cheese on 1 side of each tortilla. Layer each tortilla with 3 slices of the turkey, 3 slices of the cheese and 1/2 of the shredded carrot. Roll to enclose the filling. Cut each tortilla roll into 8 slices with a serrated knife. Serve immediately. SERVES 2 TO 4

NOTE: Tasty and healthy after-school snack.

April Fool's Colorful Cupcakes

CUPCAKES

1 pound lean ground beef
1 cup (4 ounces) shredded Monterey
 Jack cheese
1/2 cup seasoned bread crumbs

3 tablespoons ketchup
1 egg, lightly beaten
1/2 teaspoon celery salt
1/4 teaspoon pepper

POTATO FROSTING

3 cups mashed potatoes
Food coloring

For the cupcakes, line 12 muffin cups with foil baking cups. Combine the ground beef, cheese, bread crumbs, ketchup, egg, celery salt and pepper in a bowl and mix well. Fill the prepared muffin cups 3/4 full. Place the muffin cups on a baking sheet. Bake at 375 degrees for 15 minutes or until cooked through.

   For the frosting, divide the mashed potatoes into 3 equal portions and place in separate bowls. Add a few drops of food coloring to each batch to create blue, yellow and pink frostings. Spread a generous dollop of each frosting on each cupcake.
MAKES 12 CUPCAKES

Pumpkin Pie Squash

Kids love this recipe and do not realize the nutritional value of the squash.

1 (2-pound) butternut squash, peeled
3 tablespoons unsweetened orange juice
2 tablespoons brown sugar
2 tablespoons maple syrup

1/2 teaspoon cinnamon
1/2 teaspoon vanilla extract
1/4 teaspoon salt
1/4 teaspoon nutmeg

Cut the squash into 1 1/2-inch pieces and steam in a steamer for 15 to 20 minutes or until tender; drain. Cool slightly. Process the squash, orange juice, brown sugar, maple syrup, cinnamon, vanilla, salt and nutmeg in a blender until smooth. Serve immediately or spoon into a saucepan and heat. SERVES 6

Apple Dumplings

2 (8-count) cans crescent rolls
2 cooking apples, peeled and each cut into 8 slices
1 cup (2 sticks) margarine, melted
1 1/2 cups sugar
1 teaspoon cinnamon
1 (12-ounce) can lemon-lime soda

Unroll the crescent roll dough and separate into 16 triangles. Place 1 apple slice on each triangle and roll from the large end to the small end to enclose. Arrange the dumplings in a single layer in a 9×13-inch baking pan.

Mix the margarine, sugar and cinnamon in a bowl and pour over the dumplings. Pour the soda over the top. Bake at 350 degrees for 45 minutes. Serve topped with ice cream, if desired. SERVES 16

Shake-and-Make Ice Cream

Ice
6 tablespoons rock salt
1 cup milk or half-and-half
2 tablespoons sugar
1/2 teaspoon vanilla extract

Fill one 1-gallon resealable plastic bag 1/2 full of ice. Add the rock salt and seal tightly. Combine the milk, sugar and vanilla in a 1-pint resealable plastic bag and seal tightly. Place the smaller bag in the larger bag and seal tightly. Shake for 5 to 7 minutes. Open the smaller bag and enjoy. SERVES 1

Banana-Orange Slush

Delightful for a summer brunch.

2 cups boiling water
1 cup sugar
1 (15-ounce) can crushed pineapple
1 (10-ounce) jar maraschino cherries, drained
1 (6-ounce) can frozen orange juice concentrate
3 bananas, sliced

Combine the boiling water, sugar, undrained pineapple, cherries, orange juice concentrate and bananas in a heatproof bowl and mix well. Chill, covered, for 24 hours, stirring occasionally. Freeze for 8 to 10 hours or until firm.

   Remove the slush mixture from the freezer 45 minutes before serving. Scrape into sherbet glasses. SERVES 12

Fishy Freezer Pops

1 cup sugar
1 (3-ounce) package blueberry gelatin
2 cups boiling water
1 cup white grape juice
Gummy sea creatures

Dissolve the sugar and gelatin in the boiling water in a heatproof bowl and stir. Cool for 2 minutes. Stir in the grape juice. Fill 10 snack-size resealable plastic bags 1/2 full of the gelatin mixture.

   Place the bags upright on the refrigerator shelf and chill until the mixture is partially set. Press the gummy sea creatures into the gelatin and freeze. To serve, make a slit in the short side of the bag and push the frozen popsicle out one bite at a time. MAKES 10 POPS

Gooey Bananas

1 banana
1 chocolate candy bar, separated into squares
Miniature marshmallows

Peel the banana and make slits at 1-inch intervals to but not through the other side of the banana. Place 1 chocolate square and 1 marshmallow in each slit. Wrap in foil and place in hot coals or grill over hot coals for 10 to 15 minutes. SERVES 1

Peanut Butter and Jelly Bars

3 cups flour
1¹/2 teaspoons salt
1 teaspoon baking powder
1 cup (2 sticks) butter, softened
1¹/2 cups sugar
2 eggs
2¹/2 cups creamy peanut butter
1 teaspoon vanilla extract
1¹/2 cups strawberry jam

Mix the flour, salt and baking powder together. Beat the butter and sugar in a mixing bowl until creamy. Add the eggs and beat until blended. Beat in the peanut butter and vanilla. Add the flour mixture gradually, beating constantly until a dough forms.

Spread ²/3 of the dough in a buttered and floured 9×13-inch baking pan and spread with the jam. Crumble the remaining dough over the top of the prepared layers. Bake at 350 degrees for 35 to 45 minutes or until golden brown. SERVES 15

NOTE: Serve warm with a glass of cold milk.

Grandma's Sugar Cookies with Butter Icing

COOKIES
2¹/₂ cups flour
1 teaspoon baking powder
¹/₂ teaspoon baking soda
¹/₂ teaspoon salt
¹/₂ cup (1 stick) butter, softened
1 cup sugar
2 eggs
1 tablespoon milk
1 teaspoon salt

BUTTER ICING
¹/₂ cup (1 stick) butter, softened
1 teaspoon vanilla extract
Confectioners' sugar

For the cookies, sift the flour, baking powder, baking soda and ¹/₂ teaspoon salt into a mixing bowl and mix well. Add the butter, sugar, eggs, milk and 1 teaspoon salt to the flour mixture and beat until blended. Shape the dough into a ball and wrap in waxed paper. Chill for 2 hours or longer.

Roll the dough ¹/₈ inch thick on a lightly floured surface. Cut with a cookie cutter dipped in flour. Arrange 2 inches apart on a greased cookie sheet. Bake at 425 degrees for 10 minutes. Cool on the cookie sheet for 2 minutes. Remove to a wire rack to cool completely.

For the icing, beat the butter and vanilla in a mixing bowl until blended. Add the desired amount of confectioners' sugar gradually, beating constantly until creamy and of a spreading consistency. If the icing becomes too thick, add a small amount of milk and beat until blended. Spread some of the icing on each cookie.
MAKES 2¹/₂ DOZEN COOKIES

No greater joy exists for a child than the announcement of bringing home an "A." Excellent schools that afford many students an opportunity to excel bless the Owensboro-Daviess County community. The elementary schools have attracted national attention, even earning a spotlight on the "Today" show. Former President Clinton toured one of the schools as an example of educational excellence.

With forty-two elementary and secondary schools and five colleges and universities in the community, our homes have opportunities to showcase many "A's."

Edible Play Dough

1 cup creamy peanut butter
1 cup light corn syrup
1¼ cups nonfat dry milk powder
1¼ cups confectioners' sugar

Mix the peanut butter, corn syrup, milk powder and confectioners' sugar in a bowl. Knead until of the desired consistency. After playing with the dough, eat and enjoy.
MAKES FOR FUN

Popcorn Snowmen

¹/₄ cup (¹/₂ stick) butter
4 cups miniature marshmallows
9 cups popped popcorn
1 cup white chocolate morsels
Small candy-coated chocolate bits
Gumdrops
Miniature pretzel sticks
Chewy fruit snack roll-ups

Microwave the butter in a large microwave-safe bowl until melted. Add the marshmallows to the butter. Microwave on High for 1 to 2 minutes or until melted and stir with a butter-coated metal spoon until smooth. Pour the butter mixture over the popcorn in a large bowl and toss to coat.

With damp hands, form 8 balls about 3 inches in diameter, making the bases flat. Then form 8 balls about 2 inches in diameter for the top sections of the snowmen.

Microwave the white chocolate morsels in a microwave-safe dish on Medium for 1 minute or until melted; stir. Use the white chocolate as an adhesive to stack the popcorn balls together and to attach the chocolate bits for eyes, gumdrops for noses and hats, pretzel sticks for arms and cut-up roll-ups for scarves. To make hats, cut the gumdrops into halves and place 1 half cut side down on a flattened gumdrop. Attach to the top of the snowmen. MAKES 8 SNOWMEN

Sugar Plum Fairy Wands

1 (10-ounce) package marshmallows
8 ounces vanilla candy coating
$^1/_4$ cup ($^1/_2$ stick) butter or margarine
6 cups crisp rice cereal
6 ($^3/_8$×12-inch) wooden dowels

Combine the marshmallows, candy coating and butter in a 6-quart microwave-safe bowl. Microwave on High for 2 minutes and stir. Microwave for 1 to 1$^1/_2$ minutes longer or until melted and stir. Add the cereal and mix well.

Press the cereal mixture over the bottom of a lightly greased 10×15-inch baking sheet with sides. Place an 8-inch star cookie cutter on the warm cereal mixture and cut with a knife around the edges of the cutter. Remove the star to a wire rack. Repeat the process. Pat the trimmings together and press into the same thickness. Repeat the process 4 more times. Cool the stars on wire racks for 1 hour.

Insert a dowel between 2 points of each star. Decorate as desired with additional melted vanilla candy coating, assorted candies and multicolored edible glitter. Tie ribbons on each dowel with thin satin ribbon. MAKES 6 WANDS

Zebra Pops

1 (16-ounce) package double-stuffed chocolate sandwich cookies
2 cups (12 ounces) vanilla or white chocolate chips
2 tablespoons shortening
32 popsicle sticks
1 cup (6 ounces) semisweet chocolate chips

Twist apart the sandwich cookies. Combine the vanilla chips and 1 tablespoon of the shortening in a microwave-safe dish. Microwave until melted and stir. Dip the end of each popsicle stick into the vanilla chip mixture and place on 1/2 of the cookie halves. Top with the remaining cookie halves.

Arrange the cookies in a single layer on a baking sheet lined with waxed paper. Freeze for 15 minutes. Reheat the vanilla chip mixture if needed and dip the frozen cookies into the mixture until covered. Return the cookies to the baking sheet and freeze for 30 minutes longer.

Microwave the semisweet chocolate chips and the remaining 1 tablespoon shortening in a microwave-safe dish until melted and stir until smooth. Drizzle the melted chocolate over the cookies. Let stand until set. Store in an airtight container.
MAKES 32 POPS

John Foreman wrote
this menu as a child.

Monster Menu

(for when you invite a monster for lunch)

Cold soup (of raw eggs) with dumplings of mud

A beaker or two of rancid old blood.

The brains of one worm cut into very small pieces

and fried for an hour in three different greases.

Stewed gizzards of lizards with crocodile eyes

Poached pickles on toast and buckets of flies.

A steaming tureen of octopus stew

Baked bunions of witches in bugaboo goo.

Fruity Lip Gloss

2 tablespoons shortening
1 tablespoon instant fruit drink mix

Mix the shortening and drink mix in a microwave-safe dish until smooth. Microwave on High for 50 seconds or until the mixture becomes a liquid. Pour into a small airtight container, such as a 35mm film container. Chill for 20 to 30 minutes or until firm. MAKES 1 LIP GLOSS

Cinnamon Ornaments

A wonderful way to create lasting holiday memories for your family.

1 cup plus 2 tablespoons cinnamon
1 tablespoon ground cloves
1 tablespoon nutmeg
3/4 cup applesauce
2 tablespoons white glue

Combine the cinnamon, cloves and nutmeg in a bowl and mix well. Stir in the applesauce and glue. Mix the applesauce mixture with your hands until smooth.

Divide the dough into 2 equal portions. Roll each portion 1/4 inch thick on a hard surface and cut with the desired cookie cutters. Make a hole in each ornament with a drinking straw. Dry the ornaments on wire racks for several days.

Attach the desired decorations with craft glue. Thread ribbon through the holes and tie the ends into bows. MAKES FOR FUN

Bathtub Finger Paint

1/3 cup cornstarch
2 tablespoons sugar
2 cups cold water
1/4 cup clear dishwashing liquid
Food coloring

Mix the cornstarch and sugar in a saucepan. Add the cold water gradually, stirring constantly. Cook over low heat for 5 minutes or until the mixture is the consistency of a smooth, almost clear gel, stirring frequently. Let stand until cool. Stir in the dishwashing liquid.

Divide the mixture equally among several containers and tint with food coloring as desired. For more vibrant colors, use food coloring paste. MAKES FOR FUN

NOTE: This paint contains dishwashing liquid, so it dissolves in water, making it perfect for bathtub finger paint.

Located on the banks of the Ohio River, the Owensboro community takes advantage of this view by hosting music and street festivals throughout the summer. The Junior League of Owensboro participates by conducting an Art Garden for the children to make crafts and have fun. During the Art Garden, kids create flowers, have their faces painted, play in shaving cream, and make hats or marble paint. Try creating a little garden in your home by spending time with your kids while making the Bathtub Finger Paint or the Cool-Shaped Crayons (both at right).

Spray Chalk

This washable spray paint can be used on sidewalks, snow, or sand.

1 cup warm water
1/4 cup cornstarch
6 to 8 drops of food coloring

Combine the warm water, cornstarch and food coloring in a large measuring cup and mix until blended. Pour the spray chalk mixture into a small spray bottle and shake. Spray as desired, shaking the bottle before each use to avoid clogging. MAKES FOR FUN

Cool-Shaped Crayons

Broken crayons
Heavy paper cups
Candy molds

Remove all paper from the crayons and sort by color in heavy paper cups. Place 1 cup of the crayons in the microwave. Microwave on High for 4 to 6 minutes or until the crayons are completely melted.

   Pour the melted crayons into candy molds. Freeze for 20 minutes or until set. Repeat the process with the remaining cups of crayons. Different colors of crayons may be melted together to make marbleized crayons. MAKES FOR FUN

Popular Wine Varieties

WINE

CABERNET SAUVIGNON	CHARDONNAY	MERLOT
A classic blended red wine that is very intense and complex and often needs to age for at least five to ten years in order to reach peak flavor condition. Aromas and flavors include black currant, blackberry, and mint.	This grape is the best-known white wine grape grown in France. The wine made from it is often aged in small oak barrels to produce strong flavors and aromas, such as apple, lemon, vanilla, and butter.	A common grape widely grown in the Bordeaux region of France that produces a wine that is very similar to cabernet sauvignon, with which it is sometimes blended, but is usually not so intense, with softer tannins. It is not aged as long as a cabernet sauvignon.
PINOT NOIR	SYRAH/SHIRAZ	ZINFANDEL
The premier grape of the Burgundy region of France. It produces a red wine that is lighter in color than the Bordeaux reds, such as cabernet and merlot. Cherished aromas and flavors often detected are cherry, mint, and raspberry.	The syrah/shiraz is called syrah in the United States, France, and other countries. In Australia, it is called shiraz. Shiraz is known for its spicy blackberry, plum, and peppery flavors, but the syrah is slow to mature and takes on characteristics of sweet blackberries, black currants, and plums.	A grape species common to Southern Italy. An important grape variety grown in California that is used to produce robust red wine as well as the very popular blush wines called white zinfandel. Zinfandel is noted for its peppery, fruit-laden, berry-like aroma and taste characteristics in its red version, and pleasant strawberry reminders when made into a blush wine.

Popular Cheese Varieties

CHEESE

ASIAGO—Italian cheese that has a very firm texture and grates easily. Grate over pasta or pizzas or include in omelets and serve with cabernet sauvignon.

BRIE—A very soft cheese that is an excellent selection to complement a fruit tray. When heated, it makes the perfect spread for crackers or bread. Serve with a chardonnay.

FETA—A very popular salad cheese. This classic Greek cheese is readily available in the United States. Feta is a great addition to a variety of dishes and pairs well with a merlot.

GORGONZOLA—An Italian blue cheese that is creamy when young and then ages into a sharp, crumbly cheese. Toss in your favorite green salad and top with sliced pears and toasted walnuts and serve with a glass of Chardonnay.

GRUYÈRE—Excellent cheese to incorporate in hearty pasta dishes. Melt and use in sauces, soups, and fondue. Serve with a syrah or chardonnay.

MOZZARELLA—Fresh mozzarella is soft and stored in water. It is best served sliced with fresh basil, fresh tomatoes, and balsamic vinegar. One of the most popular cheeses, the fresh variety is much different that the shredded pizza-style mozzarella cheese. Serve with pinot noir.

PARMIGIANO-REGGIANO—Aged Italian cheese with a buttery flavor. Grate over pizzas, pasta dishes, or mashed potatoes. This is a cheese lover's dream come true. Goes well with any and all wine.

Wine Glossary

AROMA—The actual scent of the fruit or flower of a wine.

BALANCE—No one element—sweetness, acidity, or tartness—prevails in a wine.

BOUQUET—The rich fragrances that a wine gives off.

CRISP—Acidity levels are in balance, resulting in a fresh taste.

FRUITY—The specific aromas and flavors of the grapes are immediately evident.

FULL-BODIED—Wine with weighty, substantial flavor and a higher alcohol content.

MUST—The thick stew of juice, skins, and other matter after the crushing of the grapes.

NOSE—The combination of aroma and bouquet.

OAKY—The scent or flavor of wine aged in small oak barrels.

TANNIN—A bitter compound found in the seeds, stems, and skins of grapes.

TART—Wine with a high acidity level.

181

Recipe Contributors and Testers

Faygie Allen

Jean Allen

Joy Allen

Carson Andersen

Karen Andersen

Lily Andersen

Sandy Andersen

Jenny Anderson

Wanda Anderson

Dana Armstrong

Barbara Artrip

Pat Ashley

Andrea Austin

Mike Austin

Mignon Backstrom

Camilla Baker

Tia Barnett

Kim Belcher

Kim Bell

Janet Berger

Carol Bivins

Heather Blackburn

Jennifer Blair

Kerri Bradley

Jackie Brown

Lou Brown

Nancy Bryant

Vicky Buchanan

Becki Burton

Robin Byars

Trisha Caldwell

Casey Callis

Kristin Callis

Jane Campbell

Laurie Campbell

Paula Canant

Sherry Carpenter

Stacey Carter

Cathy Cecil

Christy Chaney

Joyce Chapman

Andre Clark

Peggi Clark

Tonya Clark

Dorothy Clary

Linda Clary

Heather Clemens

Peggy Clifton

Sophia Clifton

Voyd Clifton

Pam Collignon

Nikki Conley

Cheryl Cooper

Chris Covington

Isabella Cowan

Judy Cowan

Stacey Cowan

Erica Crabtree

Patsy Crady

Jane Crewse

Linda Crume

Nancy Cutliff

Karen Danhauer

Tracey Danzer

Daviess County Extension
  Office

Phyllis Dobbs

Sue Draper

Kerrie Druen

Carol Ecleberry

Renee Ekbladh

Christy Ellis

Hadley Embry

Heather Estes

Jason Estes

Jennifer Eubanks Wilson

Jan Evans

Ashley Ferguson

Angela Fleischmann

Ann Floyd

Kathy Fort

Jana Beth Francis

Bonita French

Stephanie Frey

Recipe Contributors and Testers

Dianne Fuqua

Ginny Futvoye

Cate Gaddis

Terrell Garrett

Rosie Gentry

Vivian Gentry

Waynetta Gentry

Michele George

Kristina Ghosal

Rebecca Glenn

Kathy Godby

Stacy Goddard

Michelle Goetz

Rhonda Goetz

Leslie Greenwood

Sandra Hagan

Christy Hall

Gay Ann Harney

Hadley Harrington

Nicole Harris

Judy Hatfield

Lois Hausner

Christy Hayden

Natalie Hayden

Sherry Hayden

Kris Hayes

Karen Head

Dina Hearn

David Hemingway

Mary Grace Hemingway

Sara Hemingway

Will Hemingway

Robin Henry

Michelle Hickerson

Jennifer Higdon

Rachel Higdon

Carly Hooper

Debbie Horton

Doug Hubbard

John Hubbard

Judy Hubbard

Julia Hubbard

Cindy Hudson

Sid Hudson

Leslie Hughes

Sara Hulse

Shannon Hulse

Jamie Hutchinson

Lisa Hyland

Jenny Inman

Mary Jane Inman

Ashlie Iracane

Ronda Iracane

Jerry Johnson

Ruth Johnson

Sean Johnson

Sherri Johnson

Jennifer Jones

Sylvia Jones

Cindy Joseph

Jamie Kelley

Wade Kelley

Ann Kendrick

Kim Kingsley

Kathy Kirk

Heather Lane

Lane Langford

John Lashbrook

Kim Lashbrook

Helen Lawton

Mimi LeClaire

Harrison Lee

Heather Lee

Hunter Lee

Carl Lewis

Claire Lewis

Clayton Lewis

Dorothy Lewis

Kim Lewis

Regina Lewis

Robin Locher

Kim Logan

Chris Love

Daniel Love

Recipe Contributors and Testers

Helen Love
Jessica Love
Michelle Love
Stephanie Luckett
Joyce Lyles
Cindy Lyons
David Lyons
Emily Lyons
Jennifer Lyons
Lindsey Lyons
Nancy Malone
Bonnie Marks
Patti May
James Mayfield
Michelle Mayfield
Ruth Mayfield
Debbie McCoy
Kim McElwain
Carolyn McKee
Carolyn McKelvey
McNulty Family
Karen Mellon
Marilyn Mercer
Kathy Miles
Fred Miller, Jr.
Mary Dean Miller
Stephanie Miller
Cindy Miracle

Linda Mock
Tracy Mohon
Ann Moore
Charlotte Moore
Patti Moore
Shelia Moore
Anne Moseley
June Mullins
Thurlene Mullins
Britnee Murphy
Gail Murphy
Jim Murphy
Sharon Murphy
Shelly Murphy
James Naas
Paula Naas
Amy Nave
Nathan Nunley
Suzette Nunley
Christina O'Bryan
Susie Overdyke
Mary Owen
Michelle Parker
Tricia Patterson
Lisa Paul
Ron Paul
Caroline Payne
Lynnette Perkins

Roxy Perkins
Angie Peters
Brock Peterson
Terri Petzold
Victoria Petzold
Brenda Phelps
Karen Plain
Jodi Pope
Judith Pope
Ann Powers
Rhonda Priest
Shannon Raines
Elizabeth Ray
Sheri Reeves
Emily Reynolds
Char Rhoads
Chris Rhoads
Clayton Rhoads
Marilyn Rhoads
Misty Rhoton
Tammy Rice
Jennifer Rickard
Jennifer Riney
Marilyn Riney
Cathy Ringham
JoAnn Risner
Lori Roberts
Robin Roberts

Recipe Contributors and Testers

Tony Roberts
Valarie Roberts
Sherry Rode
Judith Romans
Janet Rumohr
Neil Rumohr
Lee Runyon
Laura Russelburg
Nancy Ryan
Elissa Sanders
Aimee Sanders-Garrard
Evelyn Schell
Janice Schell
Robert Schell
Amy Schertzinger
Maureen Schriner
Karissa Shelton
Melissa Shelton
Kristi Sigers
Sandra Sigers
Mary Silvert
Sonya Simpson
Dina Smith
Karen Smith
Piny Smith
Peggy Stemle
Jan Sterett
Linda Stone

Cissy Sullivan
Lisa Sullivan
Doris Sumner
Camilla Sympson
Jamie Szetela
Jim Szetela
Camilla Taylor
Deborah Taylor
Katherine Taylor
Lucy Taylor
Menisa Taylor
Rachel Taylor
Ada Thompson
Elizabeth Tripp
Allison Truett
Jean Tucker
Susie Tyler
Amy Waggener
Teresa Wallace
Julie Warren
Sans Washington
Ann Watson
Ann Lawton Watson
Katrina Watts
Katherine Weisbrod
Janet Westmoreland
Gayle Wible
Anne Wightman

Amy Wilkins
Jean Williams
Kim Williams
Martie Williams
Tammy Williams
Christine Willis
Beth Wilmes
Jenny Wilson
Kelly Wiman
Lynn Wiman
Amy Windley
Pam Wise
Angela Woosley
Ken Woosley
Brenda Yeand
Jean Yeand
Joseph Yeand
Prudie Young
Meredith Zengel
Monica Zengel
Wade Zengel

Index

Index

Index

Index

Index

Index

Home Again, Home Again

OPEN THE DOOR TO OUR COLLECTION OF SOUTHERN FAVORITES

The Junior League of Owensboro
P.O. Box 723
Owensboro, Kentucky 42302-0723
270-683-1430
www.juniorleagueofowensboro.com

YOUR ORDER	QTY	TOTAL
Home Again, Home Again at $22.95 per book		$
Kentucky residents add 6% sales tax		$
Shipping at $3.50 for 1st book; $1.50 for additional books		$
	TOTAL	$

Name _____

Address _____

City _____ State _____ Zip _____

Telephone _____

E-mail _____

Method of Payment: [   ] MasterCard   [   ] VISA
                    [   ] Check payable to the Junior League of Owensboro

Account Number _____ Expiration Date _____

Cardholder Name _____

Signature _____

Photocopies accepted.